T0348303

Treasures
of
Beachcombing

Details and accounts of beachcombing in
Victoria, Tasmania, South Australia and more...

KEN MARTIN

Bas Publishing
PO Box 335
Dromana Vic 3936
mail@baspublishing.com.au
www.baspublishing.com.au

This book has been compiled by beachcombers as a guide as to what's to see around our southern coastline. Beaches and coastline as well as jetties can be dangerous. If you venture to any of these areas take extra care.

The National Library of Australia Cataloguing-in-Publication entry:

Creator:	Martin, Ken, author.
Title:	Treasures of beachcombing : details and accounts of beachcombing in Victoria, Tasmania, South Australia and more / Ken Martin.
ISBN:	9781921496387 (hardback)
Subjects:	Beachcombing--Australia.
	Beachcombing--Victoria--Anecdotes.
	Beachcombing--Tasmania--Anecdotes.
	Beachcombing--South Australia--Anecdotes.
Dewey Number:	796.530994

Front cover: Remains of a jetty, Great Ocean Road, Victoria
Back Cover: Driftwood at Pebble Beach, Mt Martha, Victoria

Also by the same author:
Walks of Flinders Island
Walks of King Island
Walks of the Shipwreck Coast and Volcano Country
Walks of the Surfcoast
Walks of the Mornington Peninsula

Proofreading: Jean Basile
Publisher: Sam Basile
Layout and design: Ben Graham
Images: Ken Martin unless otherwise acknowledged

Contents

Beachcombing

Find a remote and desolate shoreline, perhaps a rocky coastline or sandy beach. Access this seashore initially by vehicle, then foot, boat or bike and keep your fingers crossed. Any sign of recent footprints will dampen the spirits but often, the further you hike along inaccessible coastline, then the less likelihood there will be of finding any traces of human endeavour. Once a find has been noted and perhaps hidden for the return journey pickup, (why carry your booty further than is necessary?) then you will know that you are upon 'virgin' coast – a shoreline which has seen many a tide come and go since people have frequented the location now before you! If you are fortunate enough to visit small offshore islands which abound in Bass Strait, it may be months and months since anyone has scoured the coastline – what treasures lurk hidden in a nook or cranny is anyone's guess. Herein lies the excitement of the unknown. It's far better than waiting for your numbers to come up in the lottery – here along the coast you have more control and even finding small and relatively insignificant items can quickly signal to the ever-vigilant beachcomber that a bigger find is possibly just along the next section of coast.

Stunning coastline, Flinders Island.

WHO AND WHAT IS A BEACHCOMBER?

Beachcombers of yesteryear 'combed' the beaches for flotsam and debris, perhaps from shipwrecks and any items of nautical origin which might have had some value. There was the idea that one could eek out a living by beachcombing, by selling these found items. There was some association with criminal activity, whether it be by luring sailing ships onto the shore with bogus fires and lights, only to pilfer their cargo or selling ill-begotten gains from shipwrecks that clearly belonged to the owners and crew of such ill-fated vessels.

Nowadays, beachcombers do not depend on the earnings that could be generated by found items. Beachcombers are more likely to collect interesting items. Sea shells have had appeal for centuries. Would you be surprised to learn that serious nautilus shell collecting has rewarded the 'professional beachcomber' with an income' in excess of $10,000. This was when these shells were valued at around $10. Today's spot price is more likely to be $25 each. Driftwood used for building furniture and sculpture has its uses. Items lost by recreational boats and fishing vessels all have their uses and invariably a dollar value can be attributed to such items. I had heard of a found radio beacon, belonging to a long-line fishing trawler, being re-united with its owner for a reward of $500. Picking up 75 litres of diesel fuel in three plastic containers, I can vouch for the usefulness and value of some of these 'beach-combed' items. Buoys, one of my favourite 'finds',will always have a place and a value for interested collectors. One thing is certain. Serious beachcombing is a recreational activity. It connects one with the sea and the elements. 'Mother nature' is much closer when beachcombing is undertaken. I like the Wikipedia statement that 'people beachcomb to achieve better emotional, physical and spiritual health.'

Let's be precise, beaches are not combed, well not under normal circumstances. Sure, a keen lookout is kept for any signs of a valuable find.

A good pair of binoculars is an essential aid to the semi-professional. Often time can be saved by gaining high ground atop a sand dune of a headland and scanning the forward coast to check for signs of booty and interesting objects. Even distorted and unusually weathered driftwood can be a great source of satisfaction to a seasoned coastal marauder. A coastal marauder, a scavenger, a beach walker: there are many descriptions befitting a collector of sea-seasoned objects. And with the rise in prominence of all things coastal and beach-derived, such as beach-inspired home décor, beach fashions and the like, the status of the beachcomber has risen significantly.

Beaches are an Australian icon. We are identified as a nation by our huge and attractive coastline. Anyone who chooses to trek these iconic places of our national identity is instantly identified as a being a 'free and roving spirit', and is indirectly associated with the bush swagman of yesteryear. A coastal swagman! Herein is one of the strongest reasons for beachcombing. The connection with finding something for free. Not being encumbered to the 'civilized world' of regulations, of roads and signage or hoardings, as one Bass Strait islander is want to say.

Most beaches are simply repositories of mother nature's storehouse and 'Davy Jones Locker'. They serve as the last stop for items which have 'been at sea'. Sadly, along the shores of my hometown beach, southeast of Melbourne we have a mechanical beach-cleaning monster that regularly 'combs' the beach for debris and seaweed and the occasional syringe. While the principal of a tidy and clean beach is admirable, the sand certainly becomes a more sterile habitat so that any life either under the sand or shorebirds foraging for food on the tide line are severely restricted in what they may find.

So if you want to do some serious foraging along the coast, find an unspoilt, unswept coastline where mechanical monsters are non-existent.

What is the motivation for beachcombing and looking for flotsam, jetsam, lagan and buoys? There are picturesque bays, the tempest of a restless ocean, a walk on a desolate shore, being alone with nature and the ever present challenge of finding something of value, whether it be a uniquely shaped and sculptured piece of driftwood or something with a more natural origin, perhaps the body of some deceased sea-dwelling animal which could be displayed in your own 'museum of natural history.'

Exercise and a coastal walk (not being a bushwalk!) along a remote and majestic slice of coastal geomorphology can have a wow factor. Where the Killiecrankie 'mountain range' defiantly meets the sea in eastern Bass Strait, is a case in point. Old Man's Head, a 100 metre phallic prominence stands up to the storm force winds that regularly lash this rocky coastline. The shipwreck coast with its insurmountable cliffs never fail to produce feelings of awe and wonderment.

I like the coast. I walk the coast, I've surfed the coast. I dive and go boating around the coastline. We live by the sea, albeit a more sterile coastline which goes by the misnomer, Port Phillip Bay. Our bay beach is relatively free of interesting objects although from time to time, we have seen krill, nautilus shells, dinghies, buoys and ropes as well as diving gear all washed up onto the shore.

Make no mistake, Port Phillip Bay is an enormous bay. Yachties who have been 'lost' describe the 'bay' like the Pacific Ocean. At times it is almost impossible to see from one side of the bay to the other side when you're out there in the middle. We could rename Port Phillip Bay, Port Phillip Sea or Port Phillip Embayment. Getting seriously into beachcombing, a knowledge of storms, ocean currents and seasonal events can all increase the possibility of finding something of interest.

LOCATING BOOTY, BUOYS, FISH, ROPES, TIMBER, MARINE, WETSUITS...

Serious beachcombing requires time, fitness and agility, a keen eye and a minimum amount of hiking gear to make the expedition enjoyable. For an all-day hike, a large backpack with the requisite lunch, first aid kit, map, water, mobile, rain coat, pocket knife, etc. will all ensure that your efforts are made easier and that there is ample room to carry any booty which is found en route. For the serious and technically minded semi-professional beachcomber add a hacksaw, a very sharp knife and even some cable ties to strap on your booty. A PLB (Personal Locator Beacon) can add a measure of safety and even a PFD lightweight yoke is not beyond reason. The more gear I take the more confident I am at going it alone and into remote places.

Herein lies a beachcomber's collection, amassed over many years, of some of the better examples of what the oceans have spat forth on many a desolate shoreline along the coastline of south eastern Australia. With five buoys in my collection having originated from Argentina, I can truly claim to have an international collection courtesy of the mighty Southern Ocean.

Beaches

We all have our own favourite beach for swimming, sailing, surfing, diving, boating and fishing. The beachcombers favourite beach will invariably be remote, beautiful and with interesting flotsam and jetsam the one essential feature. A beach may basically identify who you are and what you do. Or is it what you'd like to do? We dream of places we'd rather be. The world's best beaches invariably draw us to a tourist mecca, if not overrun with humanity, certainly heading towards the more populous end of the scale.

There are the obligatory resorts and all things tourist – facilities: Arrh! Are these beaches relaxing? Are they the quintessential 'Australian beach'? Probably not.

Proper beaches: They are remote, desolate, inspiring, relaxing, picturesque, partially protected, wide sandy flats at low tide, a creek to add interest, rocks nearby for variety, good for walking, running, cycling and strollers. Scenic backdrop of hills and coastal geology.

Finding a drift card at the end of my patch of sand, swimming its entire length, catching fish and diving for crays as well as finding driftwood and ropes. Here's a beach that offers plenty. Having the strong endorsement of a locals' observation that 'this is the prettiest part of Bass Strait'. My thoughts turn to Killiecrankie Bay in eastern Bass Strait. Camping there for over 20 years and still camping there every year, here's a beach with awesome scenery. Friendly waves, good fishing, sheltered moorings and a sufficiently small village where locals all know one another by name and say 'Hi' on the beach. This beach is ever changing. Sunrises and sunsets, moonrises over the mountain, all can put on a spectacular show when conditions are right.

The release, the freedom, the wilderness, the untamed coast and the mighty Southern Ocean feeding into Bass Strait. This is a grand scene beyond the daily human experience of living in cities and suburbia, concrete and asphalt, with lots of houses and buildings all in a row. Everything reproduced everything the same.

How we yearn to escape the dreary, the routine and the sameness of our lives in an urban context. We will always seek the relaxation and contentment, the uncluttered nature and the lack of humanity's footprint that can be found on a beach. Kids will instantly be drawn to a rock pool at low tide, there to turn over a rock and discover a crab. Perhaps to simply wade in a small rock pool that offers security to young children. Your beach may offer the challenge of rock-hopping, of seeing juvenile fish feeding on an in-coming tide or simply good for sun-baking (Slip, slop, slap, seek and slide) and relaxing with a good book, a barbecue or a picnic.

Beaches are deeply embedded in the Australian psyche, international visitors tell us as much, and they allow us to dream and scheme of walks, of boating trips and yachting adventures, of diving and surfing expeditions to these distant shores. The way we cope with the humdrum is to put a lighthouse in front of us in the form of a beach, our favourite beach, which will show us the way through the trials and tribulations of our urban lives. With the coldness of winter we rug up and tackle the seriously impinging wind chill factor. Consider at Cape Grim in 2011, with 8°C air temperature and 140 km per hour wind gusts, the wind chill was around minus 12°C.

And winter water temperatures of 12C also require serious wetsuits

Mornington Peninsula National Park, Victoria.

Isolated sandy cove, Bass Strait.

and associated gear for activities such as surfing and diving. One wetsuit manufacturer had an electric element in their wetsuits to keep the surfer warm. Abalone (ab) divers are known to have hot water pumped into their suits in order to keep them down on the seabed to earn a living. Many thousands of Australians simply say at home.

But the summer always comes. Tens of thousands of us hit the beaches. What are the best beaches? The best beach is the one you frequent. It doesn't matter if your favourite beach is not among the top 50 beaches in the world. Beaches are our birthright. In Australia they form part of our national identity. Just ensure it's a patrolled beach if you are going into the water, please.

Bottles

It's amazing what you can find swimming and diving around jetties, and along the sandy beaches. My best finds have occurred as a result of weekly swims at Portsea pier. This allows a good chance to observe the sea floor which has been home to boats, holidaymakers and visitors for well over a hundred years. A lemonade bottle, complete with marble, 'G. Hibbert and Son, Sorrento', was a great find in the autumn of 2011. Even a summer swim in the shallows at Rosebud resulted in finding a White Crow tomato sauce bottle albeit with a small hole on one side. The purple tinge of the glass indicated that it was many years old, this coloration being the result of long term exposure to UV light. Broken, water-worn glass of many colours has been collected and placed in layers in bigger glass bottles with great effect.

Old pieces of slate near the site of the derelict jetty at Lillies Bay, Tasmania are an easy find and they also reinforce the local history that is part of the makeup of this part of the world.

The waters adjacent to the Quarantine Station at Point Nepean National Park, Victoria, occasionally reveal old plates and dinner ware, albeit mostly

G. Hibbert & Son Sorrento found near
Portsea Pier, Victoria.

Old Bottle from under Portsea Pier, Victoria.

broken pieces, for those prepared to look. This is precisely where the doomed immigrant ship, the Ticonderoga came to be moored in December, 1852. One hundred passengers died on the voyage after a deadly outbreak of typhus. Many more passed away at what is now a very interesting historical site. Warning: Those thinking of swimming at Ticonderoga Bay and diving in this area need to be aware of the strong tidal current at this location, being less than five kilometres from 'the rip', the notorious water way that is the entrance to Port Phillip Bay. Swimming and snorkelling around any part of our coastline may just reveal a long-hidden treasure, waiting to be found by the observant collector.

Buoys

Buoy: n. 1. an anchored float serving as a navigation mark or to show reefs, etc. 2. a lifebuoy v.tr. 1. (usu. foll. by up) a) keep afloat b) sustain the courage or spirits of (a person, etc.); uplift, encourage. 2 (often foll. by out) mark with a buoy or buoys.

The need for navigational infrastructure developed with the emergence of maritime trade and today, mariners in unfamiliar waters keep a sharp lookout for lighthouses, buoys, beacons and other navigational aids as they approach harbours, anchorages and moorings. Lighthouses have been the prominent and pre-eminent navigational aid for mariners for many hundreds of years. With digital technology and satellites, a new age has arrived whereby what is old is invariably obsolete.

But buoys, with a history dating back to at least the 13th century in European waters, have had an enduring association with mariners and seafarers for all this time. The first recorded buoy was located in Spain, in the Guadalquivir River. This particular buoy aided mariners approaching the port of Sevilla by its identifying the safest course up the mouth of the river.

Records of buoys from yesteryear and early buoyage history are yet to be

Argentinean buoy made in South America washed
in at Fingal Beach, Cape Schanck, Victoria.

Found booty from near Millers Bay, King Island.

Barnacle bill buoy, Sisters Passage, Eastern Bass Strait.

finalized. Suffice is to say that simple floatation devices, perhaps casks and spars, formed an early part of the infrastructure of these simple navigational aids. Standardization of buoyage with respect to colour, size and shape came a little later in the evolutionary tree of navigational aids. Today buoys still have a multitude of uses: from identifying mooring and craypots to floating nets and associated fishing gear, buoys are indispensable. The soft buoys are excellent boat fenders, the older ones have 'collectors' appeal and 'as new' buoys can sometimes be traded for other goods and services from your friendly local fisherman.

Cleaning your buoys. Sandy beaches seem to have a propensity to wash up the cleanest buoys and fishing floats. Ocean sands offer a clean environment and the tumbling action on a berm or shore break usually results in a good clean float. People who have an outside shower may simply like to get a laundry scrubbing brush and give the offending debris a 'what for' as you shower away the salt from your persona.

But on rocky shores perhaps with clay impregnated cliffs, such as is found along the shipwreck coast in Victoria, the buoys can become contaminated with soil and the 'froth and bubble' found in a gulch or along a creek, where the sea foam covers your find with a fine coating of debris, initially making for a poor specimen. Smelly barnacles can add a challenge to buoy collectors if the buoy has been washed up high and dry for some time and left to bake in the summer sun.

The solution: place your buoy or surface float in a large plastic bin and soak for 1 to 24 hours, depending on the severity of the grime, then with a laundry scrubbing brush start to scrub vigorously. Be sure to scrub along each individual rope if you are cleaning a rope-netted plastic buoy. Apart from getting rid of grime and any algae, minute organisms will be washed away and there should be no smell of marine animal life left to spoil your good find.

And don't stop when you go overseas. International 'collections' are sure to

Buoy recovered from wreck, Inner Sister Island.

Glass buoy and rope found near Old
Mans Head, Flinders Island Tasmania.

Buoys washed in at The Crags, via
Warrnambool, Western Victoria.

Glass Float

Location: Swain's Reef, Great Barrier Reef, Queensland
Date: 1980's
Type: Glass float with tar impregnated rope weave
Size: 295mm diameter
Use: Trawl fishery
Features: Relatively rare and in short supply
Country of origin: Japan
Stamped features: Nil
Price: From $5 at a garage sale to in excess of $200. Keep under lock and key. Check out eBay and similar web-based outlets for current prices and locations.

One of my prized possessions, this particular float was traded with a work colleague for a whale vertebra many years ago. The staffer's husband worked for the Department of National Mapping and he would find himself in far-flung and distant locations, in this case on a coral atoll, where there were three of these rather unique floats.

add an element of intrigue and interest for diehard collectors and observers: 'where on earth did you get that from?' Ensure your buoys are 'clean skins' when you pass through Quarantine, being decontaminated and scrubbed prior to departure for home. My Samui buoys (Gulf of Thailand), over 25 in number, add a source of interest to my collection. They are extremely lightweight and almost flimsy, indicating the calmer seas that the region experiences for most of the year.

eBay may surprise you with the price sellers are asking for glass floats, cork fishing net floats and even the heavy duty plastic buoys encased with rope weave.

The impressive La Coruna aluminium water depth buoy was offered on bidbuy.co.zaB listed for 400 Rand with a market value of 1200 Rand. Is AU $200 too much for this piece of history?

A word of etiquette for keen collectors. If you happen upon fishing gear such as ropes, buoys and lines that may be connected to or owned by a local fisherman then enquire as to the rightful owner. This is particularly relevant if there are registration numbers on the buoys. (See the section titled: Law of the Sea.) I was embarrassed a few years ago when I found some gear on the beach and I proceeded to walk off with gear which had the same registration numbers as a boat moored nearby.

GLASS FLOATS

Glass floats or buoys are in a class all of their own. With a history dating back to Norway in the 1840's, these 'Rolls Royce' items are a sure find on any collectors or decorators 'want to find' list. Japanese fisherman used these types of floats for many years. Consequently, it is said that they are still in reasonable supply, albeit in the northern Pacific Ocean.

The biggest 'loss', the one that got away, occurred at Low Point on the northern tip of Flinders Island Tasmania. Conducting a bushwalking camp and doing a coastal trek, one member of our group happened across the 'real McCoy', complete with rope and an unblemished glass ball. I have duly applied for future salvage rights, lest he relinquishes ownership.

Crays, Cray Pots and Cray Measures

Beachcombing for crays? If you walk far enough and long enough around the coast you will come across a broken shell or leg of these 'red sheep' as one fisherman calls his crays. Further expeditions may even reveal a broken cray pot washed up on the beach or the rocks. If you are really lucky you may find a complete craypot in tact. There was one such pot, albeit in four metres of water, washed into the shallows, off Rye ocean beach, on Melbourne's famed Mornington Peninsula.

To see 'crayfish' action, the bagging of crays for shipment to the city and overseas, an early start at your nearest wharf is recommended. Crayfish are very much a part of the sea 'scene' in this part of the world. Amateurs and professional fishermen alike chase the elusive Southern Rock Lobster. Professionals use cray pots made from a variety of materials to catch these delicacies of the deep. Traditional cray pots are usually circular and are made from cane, plastic, ti-tree and steel. The 'modern' cray pots may have red plastic necks and chicken wire or net covering a steel frame. All pots need bait holders to attract the crays. As well, an escape hatch must be fitted to all pots

Bagging crays for the market,
Killiecrankie, Flinders Island.

to allow the undersized and juvenile crays to make their way back to the open sea. Zinc anodes are often attached to the steel bases of the cray pots to inhibit corrosion.

Making cray pots the traditional way is hard work. First there is the collecting of the pot sticks in the bush. Ti-trees that are thin with new growth are easier to bend and the longer they are the better. These sticks are steamed in a long steel cylinder and when they are pliable they are woven into the wire frame of the cray pot with considerable dexterity. A good deal of strength is required to bend the 6mm galvanized rods or wire into shape for the craypot and its base.

Being a 'decky' or deckhand on a cray boat is challenging and it can be hard and repetitive work. As the boat heads out to the open sea, the deck hand cuts up the bait, frozen or fresh, and places it in bait holders, ready to attach to the pots with wire skewers. As you approach the pot buoys, the decky will throw the grab-all to catch the rope and then place it on the pot hauler. The crew and skipper look to the pot as it breaks the surface. How many crays did we catch? The 'fish' are then placed in the well, a holding tank full of seawater, to keep the crayfish alive, prior to returning to shore.

Crayfish measures are an integral part of maintaining the fishery. These items are essential for amateur and professional fisherman alike as they prevent the harvesting of undersized crayfish, thus insuring the long term survival of the resource. Plastic has superseded the bronze cray measures which are still available for sale throughout tackle and marine stores in Tasmania.

In Tasmania crays can be held in large, triangular, timber framed boxes which are moored at sea. Called cauffs, these containers can be towed into shore where the crays are packed into fish bins or bags ready for transport to Melbourne, Sydney, Japan and beyond.

Cray pots at Killiecrankie Bay, Flinders Island.

Crays – no need to measure. Flinders Island.

Cuttlebone and Cuttlefish

What is one of the first things you look at when you arrive at the beach? The sea of course. Then there's the sand. Any shells? Perhaps a ship or yacht can be seen on the horizon. But one of the most common pieces of sea flotsam or debris is the humble cuttlebone. That elongated and strangely elliptically- shaped white object is a ready-made boat for children and budgie food for pet lovers the world over. Cuttlebone has also been used as an antacid, for sculpturing and as a toothpaste additive.

The cuttlebone is the underrated and overlooked flotation device of the cuttlefish and it is often found above the high tide line, where it has possibly been blown, having washed in from the ocean. A prized seafood in many countries, the cuttlefish is actually a mollusc not a fish. The cuttlebone is the internal shell which is used as a flotation device. The animal is now thought to be rather intelligent with a large brain relative to its body volume.

The giant Australian cuttlefish is the largest cuttlefish in the world with males getting up towards a metre in total length. The colourful changes of hue have been noted by marine scientists who have studied this creature in the Gulf of St Vincent, South Australia. The speed of colour change and

the diversity of patterns in this animal are apparently unparalleled on planet earth. Scientists declaring that they have 'smart skin'. The eyes are also amongst the most highly developed of any animal. Keep a lookout for this amazing marine animal. For video footage visit http://www.abc.net. au/catalyst/stories where the ABC program outlines recent studies on the Australian cuttlefish.

Dinghies

The best ones are the ones you find. I have heard reports of people finding small tinnies complete with outboards, drifting in Bass Strait. I chanced to salvage a 12 foot tinny (a small aluminium boat) inside Port Phillip Bay a few years ago. Completely abandoned, I managed to get it home in the back of the ute. Only then did I discover the reason it was an 'orphan.' Scores of tiny corrosion holes were scattered about the hull. One can of body filler and more than eighty stainless steel screws, the boat was 'seaworthy' and is now is use again as a tender.

Another find was also on the shores of Port Phillip Bay, near Whitecliffs. This particular boat ended up at Rosebud Police Station where the owner was able to retrieve his dinghy. A very damaged tinny washed up on the rocks on Outer Sister Island, Furneaux Group some years ago. When we finally got ashore and inspected the wreck we reckoned it would have cost more in repairs than in buying an equivalent second hand dinghy. So there she lay, high up on the rocks.

Tinnies and row boats, inflatable boats, whatever the boat, you need a boat to boat across the waves. To dive and explore, and certainly to visit

Dinghies beached and moored, Killiecrankie Bay, Flinders Island.

20738

Dinghy abandoned from Port Phillip Bay, Victoria.

Rowing boat at Portarlington, Victoria.

Old dinghy adjacent to Currie Wharf, King Island.

offshore islands, some type of transportation is essential. Memorable boating experiences include, passing mutton birds or shearwaters with my son in our tinny which was a former abalone divers' boat. Our tinny is on the heavy side but very stable and it can scoot along very comfortably with a small load, whether it be passengers or a load of driftwood. In one instance, while out off the northeast coast of Flinders Island the mutton birds resembled a swarm of mosquitoes. Bass and Flinders on their exploratory journey through this patch of water, also encountered huge numbers of these migratory birds. They estimated over a million birds had passed them in the hour.

And then there is the 'right place right time scenario. Walking along Shelly Beach, on the southern Mornington Peninsula, a small tinny was noticed to slowly drift towards Port Phillip Heads on an ebb tide. My immediate reaction was to see if I could spot the skipper-come-fisherman on board. After a short time I reckoned this boat, at some considerable distance from shore, had no one aboard. Had the 'crew' fallen overboard? I phoned a local skipper who just happened to be driving by in his dive boat. With his mobile on message bank I opted to ring 000 and let the authorities investigate. Within minutes the Peninsula Searoad ferry came by and the skipper wheeled the ferry around, dropped the front ramp and dragged the dinghy on board. Only later did I learn that the tinny had drifted from its mooring after being hap-hazardly tied. The skipper of that same dive boat was a little embarrassed to admit that this was his boat! All ended well.

Dolphins, Whalebones and Fish Skeletons

Admired by people of all ages, dolphins are recognized as friendly and intelligent sea creatures throughout the world. Widely studied and researched, dolphins always attract a considerable amount of attention and at the southern end of Port Phillip Bay, Victoria, where a whole niche industry has emerged: dolphin swims. What's very interesting is that in mid-2011 a new species of dolphin has been identified in Port Phillip Bay. Tursiops Australis or the Burrunan Dolphin split from the common Bottle Nose dolphins 5.2 to 5.6 million years ago. Estimates indicate that there are up to 120 Baurranam Dolphins in Port Phillip Bay and around 50 in the Gippsland Lakes, Victoria. Coastal walking gives beachcombers ample opportunity to see these dolphins in action. Surfers and divers as well as boaties and yachties all get their chance to see the spectacular creature in action. One very memorable experience with dolphins occurred near the Waratah Bay camping ground

Head of Bottlenose dolphin skeleton.

Bottlenose Dolphin found at
Killiecrankie Bay, Flinders Island.

in South Gippsland, where we could clearly see the dolphins surfing on the unbroken waves. An amazing sight.

Holidaying and beachcombing on Flinders Island some years ago I came across a dolphin carcass near Diamond Gully. This bottle nose dolphin, identified by its large teeth, (The Common Dolphin has needle -like teeth) still had many large pieces of dried skin attached and it was too heavy to lift on to the dinghy for the trip back to port. Returning the next day with a hacksaw, I deftly separated the two halves with the skill of the butcher not an orthopaedic surgeon and the bi-section was done. I returned to the boat ramp offloaded my specimen and hung the two halves in a tree for two and a half years. Time and tide came and went, ants scampered about and finally the bare bones remained. Having contacted the Queen Victoria Museum in Launceston, I was assured that there was no manual about preparing such skeletons or assembling or mounting them for posterity. So after taking verbal instructions I set about scraping off the skin and cementing the loose teeth back into the jaw. Finally, and after discussions with the owners of the Lady Barren Tavern, Flinders Island, who had successively retrieved a baby pilot whale and mounted it on their hotel wall, I took their advice and gave the skeleton a coat of paint: 'bone white' if my memory serves me correctly. The theory goes that after a few years of dust and accumulated spider webs and whatever, your skeleton will look aged, authentic, but also protected from oxidization and attack by small animals.

Whale watching and all things 'whale' are a major focus in our media. Most western countries now protect and promote whale eco-tourism, where available. This is a far cry from the exploitative nature of these nations less than a century ago. Nations that still flout international opinion in pursuit of supposed 'scientific research' are increasingly on the outer of international opinion. The time is fast approaching when these predatory countries, harking back to earlier 'colonial times', will be no more. Perhaps this change in public

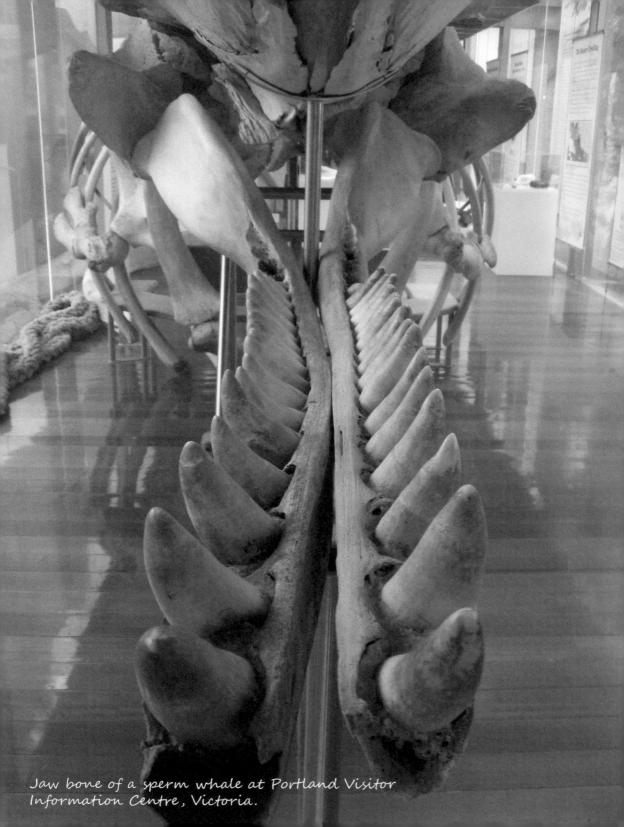

Jaw bone of a sperm whale at Portland Visitor Information Centre, Victoria.

Massive whale vertabrae,
Furneaux Museum, Flinders Island

Whale rib and vertebra recovered from
'Whalebone Cove' Eastern Bass Strait.

perception is in part due to the actions of organisations like Greenpeace and WWF, the World Wildlife Fund.

While all things whale and dolphin are protected under state and federal laws in Australia, it is a shame to see so few of the remains of these massive animals available for public display. The Blue Whale specimen that proudly takes pride of place at the Portland Visitor Information Centre is a case in point. Perhaps more assembled skeletons be made available for perusal at King and Flinders Island airports, as well as more remnants readily accessible to schools and other educational institutions. Dinosaur skeletons are always awe-inspiring at museums. In time whale skeletons may take their rightful place as enormous ambassadors for the true denizens of the deep.

A retrieved pilot whale skeleton from a school camping and bushwalking expedition to Flinders Island takes pride of place in the science wing of our secondary college. After the event we chanced to phone Tasmanian Parks Service to enquire about assembling our collection of bones. Talk of export and import permits was quickly dismissed when we were told that 'we don't have a problem with educational institutions retrieving such objects for further study.' The stranding from which this specimen derived occurred at Patriarch Inlet on the east coast of Flinders Island on the 4th of November 1980, where over 70 pilot whales were stranded. What is amazing is that many of the whales finally came to rest some 1000 metres from the beach and the mouth of the inlet. An excellent specimen, a young juvenile pilot whale, can be seen in the bar of the Furneaux Tavern and Hotel at Lady Baron, Flinders Island.

Fish Skeletons And Carcasses. If you want to start your very own museum of all things 'marine and sea', this is the place to start. Watch out for the smelly ones. Let me explain. I can still see the wooden window frame of our new house in the foothills of Melbourne, freshly painted olive green. The smell and the etching of the paintwork that occurred after a 'not quite dry' marine

Whale skeleton Patriarch Inlet, Flinders Island.

Leather Jacket, Martha Point, Victoria.

Leafy Sea Dragon and Georgian Fan from
Gosses Reef Flinders Island.

Star gazer found adjacent to Killiecrankie
Creek, Flinders Island.

organism, a sea shell, was placed on the window sill is easily recalled. As collectors do, you bring home from the sea all your booty and finds and proudly display them to all and sundry. This one 'find' was what we call today, NQR, or not quite right. The 'juices' slowly oozed out from the shell and the smell was well beyond the capacity of a room freshener. So if you do collect these items, dry them outside first, absolutely check that all is ok before bringing them into the house.

My prized possession here is the stargazer. A fearsome looking fish at the best of times, they apparently make for good eating. My large and gruesome looking specimen was found at the mouth of Killiecrankie Creek, Flinders Island, one of my favourite summer haunts. After the drying process was complete, leaving it out in the sun, I set about to give it a coat of white acrylic paint. This not only gives the fish a uniform colour but also preserves the skin and cartilage from insect and bug attack and atmospheric decay.

Fossicking for fish is best done over the summer months with higher daytime temperatures and collectors may be more productive on rocky coastlines, above the high tide line. Be sure to keep your specimens outside until they are thoroughly dried and 'cured'.

Diving Gear

O ver the years there have been substantial changes in diving gear. Both scuba diving (self contained underwater breathing apparatus) and skin-diving, now known by the 'upmarket' term 'free diving', are evolving in terms of equipment. Generally, diving gear has become more durable, more compact and certainly more high tech. Just take the example of the split fins (seal-like twin blades on each fin) The Oceanic V12 split fin claims to be up to 40% more efficient than traditional fins. Almost every beachcomber will find at least one fin washed up on the beach. If you find two matching fins, you've had a very good day.

Face masks of old had an outer stainless band which has now been superseded by plastic retainers and the toughened single glass lens now vies with the deeper styled twin lens which can give better vision. Masks are an item that are easily lost and washed onto the shore. What I'd really like to find is a snorkel with the ping pong ball valve at the top. Torches are another relatively common item that get washed up onto the coast. I suspect there is a Yin and Yan of diving gear. You loose some and if you are lucky, you find some gear too.

Diving mask and torches from Bass Strait Islands.

Even spear guns are fair game. One that I located in the water, off Rye ocean beach was reconditioned into use. My best find though, in the 'blood sport' department would have to be a gun located at Blairgowrie a few years ago. Fashioned with two old wood plane handles, the 'bazooka' came complete with sights and a stainless steel spear.

Another spear gun, at 1.7 metres and called the 'Predator' is of more recent origin and is truly for the serious offshore free divers who are hunting for pelagics. Pneumatic guns have their place but it appears that the purists still like two or even three gun rubbers for maximum' bang.'

Divers torches are almost a sure find along coastlines in the Bass Strait region. Lucky beachcombers will find a 'going concern', a torch recently lost, fully watertight and still with sufficient power to run the torch light. Sadly, time and tide take their toll and there are more damaged and partially complete torch housings washed up on the sand and rocky shores. The best find on Rye ocean beach was a divers torch, fully sealed, complete with rechargeable batteries. My partner can take the credit for that one! The new technology with led lights and 'cree' leds has put to rest the big boys of the past. The old Toshiba divers torch, complete with its four D cell batteries, is laughable when compared to today's lightweight, small and compact devices.

Drift Cards: The 'Message In A Bottle'

Spawning movies like Message in a Bottle in 1998, as well as a huge hit for the rock band, Police, in 1979, this emergency form of communication has come full circle. Today mariners have EPIRB's, (emergency position indicating radio beacons) satellite communications and the universal mobile phone with which to place distress calls. Messages in bottles only work for those washed up on to some distant shore and preferably a sandy beach.

For scientific purposes and up until the advent of satellite tracking, drift cards and floating buoys were used by researchers to track ocean currents. The drift cards featured here, all found by the author, were discovered on the eastern shores of Killiecrankie Bay, Flinders Island. One of the CSIRO drift cards had floated from a release point south of Norfolk Island and the other card was released off Low Rocky Point, Southwest Tasmania, on the 12th of August 1985.

CSIRO's earliest experiments with bottles were undertaken in the late 1930s. Drifting on the eastern Australian current, one of the bottles travelled from Queensland to South Australia. In the mid-1950's bottles were released near Albany in Western Australia and located at Eucla some 15 years later, around 1000 kilometres away.

The tragic and mysterious demise of the Malaysian Airlines flight MH 370 sharply focused public attention on oceanic drift. With scores of search aircraft and vessels as well as satellite imaging used to scour the ocean for signs of the aircraft, scientists and meteorologists scrambled to predict the likely whereabouts of the missing aircraft.

Similarly the surface drift study by the South Australian Department of Fisheries, released these 'passive drifters' to provide information on water movement. These cards move under the collective action of tides and wind.

These cards were released from the Gulf of St Vincent and Investigator Strait and were used to examine the behaviour and movement of the pelagic larvae of scale fish. In this specific study the distribution of King George whiting was being investigated. More than 15,000 cards were released in 1989 and 1990 for this particular study. It is interesting to note that satellite tracked buoys were also used, one being released near Troubridge Island in June 1990 and this washed ashore south of Adelaide confirming the findings of the earlier studies.

Following in the footsteps of oceanographers and other great researchers, my son cast off a message in a bottle from Killiecrankie Bay, Tasmania, many years ago. We decided that using a plastic bottle would be best as the coastline around Flinders Island is very rocky. While a plastic bottle is certainly far less romantic it eventually stood the test of time. Some months later, and back home in Victoria we received a phone call from the finder of the bottle, a resident from the eastern suburbs of Melbourne. The bottle had drifted some 20 kilometres around the coast and was washed up on Marshall Bay, Flinders Island. Of course my son was elated. There was every chance that this one release could have blown out into the Tasman Sea and headed for New

Drift Card recovered near Old Mans Head, Bass Strait.

PLEASE RETURN
70 CENTS REWARD
DRIFT CARD
Please mail this card giving the following
information
DATE FOUND............ WHERE FOUND,
NEAREST KNOWN POST OFFICE
AND FINDERS NAME AND ADDRESS TO
C.S.I.R.O. DIVISION OF FISHERIES & OCEANOGRAPHY
P.O. BOX 21
CRONULLA, N.S.W. 2230
Nº 016397

SOUTH AUSTRALIAN
DEPARTMENT OF FISHERIES
SURFACE DRIFT STUDY
WHEN FOUND RING PETER (08) 226 0635
REVERSE CHARGES MON - FRI 9am - 5pm
OR SEND DETAILS OF LOCATION AND DATE TO:
135 PIRIE STREET, ADELAIDE.
SOUTH AUSTRALIA. 5000

Surface Drift Study, released from South Australia, found at Flinders Island.

Zealand or even South America. As discussed elsewhere, some of my prized finds have been five South American fishing buoys, from Argentina. Surely it's a fair guess to suppose, that they had drifted all the way across the Southern Ocean and into Australian territorial waters.

Interestingly the World Health Organization has determined that Australians breathe some of the cleanest air in the world. This finding is based on the measurements of PM10 – airborne particles of 10 micrometers or less. The Cape Grim atmospheric monitoring station situated on the northwest coast of Tasmania confirms these findings and the simple explanation is that there is literally nothing in the way of human habitation between the Australian landmass and continent of South America. Having found 5 buoys with Argentine markings which have presumably drifted across from South America to Australia, I certainly endorse these findings.

Driftwood, Driftwood Furniture and Deck Hatches

Driftwood comes in all shapes and sizes and it comes in many different timbers. Oregon, and pine, the occasional red gum, hardwood, macracarpa, King Billy pine, perhaps a log of the rare Huon pine and scrappy timber that defies identification but aptly befits the description of 'dunnage.' There are the oddly shaped pieces of driftwood: one shaped like the south island of New Zealand. Another piece, recovered from Green Island in eastern Bass Strait, looks for all the world like a fish. We used this specially shaped 'fish' timber as our business logo for a number years, the business being Seadrift Enterprises. And where does it originate? If not from Western Australia and from northern Australia then perhaps from South American and beyond.

Collecting driftwood, the flotsam and jetsam from ships and other sources, from around the coast sounds glamorous. Believe me it's not. The locations can be spectacular but it's hard work. Motor your dinghy for up to an hour and a half around the coast, when sea conditions are suitable. Often I've moored the dinghy 50 metres off the rocky shore, two anchors used for security, then

Major driftwood at Narrawong Beach, Western Victoria.

Bench and buoy at Rye, Victoria.

Beached table near Tyrone Forsehore boat ramp,
Port Phillip Bay, Victoria.

Big bench, Rye, Victoria.

Driftwood furniture cast adrift on Port Phillip Bay, Victoria.

Park bench on the shores of Port Phillip Bay, Victoria.

swum in, and walked over the wet rocks, which can be tricky in itself. Always keeping a check on the dinghy and any ocean swell that could cause the boat to upset. Then collect driftwood, sometimes piece by piece, before tying the timbers together and swimming back out to the boat to load up. It's always a slow trip back to port with a few hundred kilograms of wood in the dinghy. I've reckoned the all-up weight with outboard and fuel, could be up to half a tonne, heading back to port. After shipping the driftwood across Bass Strait the pallets of driftwood are then collected at Port Welshpool and driven back to the Melbourne. Phew! Then and only then does the furniture making begin.

And as a 'professional' there is the annual Driftwood Licence. Not all areas along the coast are allowed to be accessed for collecting timber and, in particular, the endangered shorebirds environment must be respected and avoided at all times. Warning: it is illegal to remove anything from a National Park. The author was fined $100 for removing driftwood from a national park some years ago. However, as there was a pending licence application the Ombudsman found in my favour. 'Professional' collectors and those using driftwood for commercial gain. ie: business use, are advised to apply for a licence.

A driftwood furniture enterprise was initially started out of necessity, crafting functional pieces for our summer camp in Tasmania. A table and seats, a sand pit for our son and a shower recess, the kitchen sink stand, which still survives today, some 20+ years later, as well as a kitchen cupboard were all fashioned out of driftwood. In the 'camping days' these items were necessities which improved our level of comfort, particularly when we were occupying the camp for a month at a time. We were so well set up at our camp that one visitor thought we 'lived' there permanently. When we moved to a shack we needed a larger kitchen table with seats as well as an outside 'picnic table' and park bench or 'lovers seat' for two. As the 'provider' for the family I was rather taken with this observation and this comment as we did have more than the

Driftwood dining table. Timbers found around the coast Furneaux Group.

usual collection of home comforts.. Over the years the driftwood furniture has appeared in newspapers, national television and local papers. At the present point in time, and due to a diminution of driftwood supplies around our coastline, there appears to be less and less driftwood: perhaps one of the disadvantages of containerization.

Later, I embarked on the idea of running a part time mini business, manufacturing driftwood furniture. As the business became commercial in nature, bureaucracy reared its head and an application for a licence to collect driftwood was duly sought. More of a reserved land licence to conduct a

Deck hatch now used as a seat. Found at Low Point, Boat Harbour Beach, Flinders Island.

Deck hatch, Roydon Island, Furneaux Group, Tasmania.

specific activity, the licence legitimizes the taking of wood along certain parts of the Bass Strait coastline.

The driftwood furniture has been taken to places as far away as Uluru, where it has been photographed. Another enthusiast purchased a park bench from a gallery in Bass Strait, then dismantled the entire piece, ready for shipment back to Melbourne.

Deck hatches: When boats were wooden, and all boats were, these items were essential pieces of equipment, covering cargo holds, engine rooms and the like. The steel handles are indicative of a time before stainless steel (corrosion resistant steel) came to the fore. It's amazing in these present times that household appliances and safety railing is all made from stainless steel, yet these older boats did not have stainless steel handles and they were constantly exposed to salt water. Some of the deck hatches displayed here have been made into seats, one for our dining table and the other as a park or lounge bench. I do not expect to find any more of these relics from the past in the coming years. They come from what is now largely a bygone era of sea transportation. Wooden ships with wooden deck hatches. With the increasing containerization of sea freight even driftwood will become more scarce as we move to a more sustainable future. Still, on a distant coastline, at some far away location, another deck hatch awaits.

East Australian Current

The Eastern Australian current originates in the tropics, The Coral Sea, and slowly winds its way down the Eastern Australian coast, past Bass Strait and into the Tasman Sea east of Tasmania. Captain Cook on his epic voyage of discovery was one of the first mariners to note the presence of this current, which is stronger during the warmer months of the year and peaks in February. Sydney to Hobart yachtsmen are said to take water temperature readings when off the southern New South Wales coast. An extra few degrees in water temperature translates into a real gain in speed as the big maxis race towards Hobart for line honours. Some web-based discussion on this current indicates speeds of up to 5 knots.

What does this mean for beachcombers along the shores and coastline of Bass Strait? Ocean debris originating in far Northern Queensland and the Pacific can wash up along the Victorian and Tasmanian coast. One C.S.I.R.O drift card I recovered from Flinders Island was jettisoned off Norfolk Island albeit some years prior to my discovery of this item. (See section on Driftcards for a detailed description.) Not surprisingly Greenback Turtles, Sunfish and other marine life based in the Great Barrier Reef can venture far south into

Driftwood and barnacles found near Narrawong, Western Victoria.

Message in a bottle. Yambuk Coastal Reserve, Western Victoria.

our southern waters. The grey coloured volcanic pumice stone can be found in Bass Strait, its origins clearly from northern waters, perhaps Papua New Guinea or the island of Vanuatu. Timber, plastic, fishing gear and all types of debris may well find its way into these southern waters and your bag of booty. Obviously, prolonged easterly winds will accelerate this trend.

Fish Bins

Fish bins do the rounds of coastal marauders and beachcombers, being an item washed overboard from the plethora of fishing boats that ply our offshore waters. Like the proverbial milk crates which are reported to go missing the rate of over $3 million per annum in Australia, fish bin 'loss' is also a very significant cost item for the fishing industry. In many cases, fish bins as well as milk crates that are washed overboard and arrive on a rocky shoreline are battered, broken and unfit for recycling back into the industry.

Plastic self-draining crates are a relatively common find along the remote shores of Bass Strait. The eastern Australian current brings warmer tropical water from far north Queensland past Sydney and into Bass Strait. True recyclers will retrieve broken bins which can be joined with rope and 'lashed' together for storage and other general uses.

In March, 2012 a fishing trawler, the Lady Cheryl, ran aground on Corsair Rock, at the entrance to Port Phillip Heads. Portsea ocean beach became littered with bins, at least the vision on the nightly news indicated as much. This time though, beachcombers were on the backburner as Parks

Get Hooked fish bin, found
at Flinders Island, Tasmania.

SYDNEY
FISH
MARKET
AUSTRALIA

Get hooked on
fresh fish

Fish bin Discovery Bay Coastal Park,
Cape Bridgewater, Victoria.

Victoria staff and fishermen collected the ill-begotten goods for return to the skipper and the trawler.

Sydney Fish Market bins are a good find too. Another unknown fishing boat lost a deck-load of gear and this became a case of 'finders keepers' for Bass Strait fishermen, although the legal position, courtesy of a 'Legal Opinion' column in a country newspaper, explains that the true owner will always have first rights to any such booty. While such items should be handed to the nearest police station, the likely-hood of any claims probably dictates a more practical solution. Similarly, milk crates present an identical problem. The true owner is clearly marked on most crates. But one crate found at Flinders Island, labelled 'Lincoln Dairies' from South Australia, makes any attempt at return futile, more so when this crate has been scuffed, abraded and generally damaged when it was washed up on the rocks.

Fishing Reels and Rods

Lost fishing reels and fishing rods can be found almost anywhere along the coast but particularly near well frequented fishing spots. Good finds have been realized under jetties and piers as well as around boat moorings. The true collectibles here are the bakelite reels, the open-casters and anything that has had some marine growth. The majority of my limited collection came from around Portsea pier, with the addition of some donated items. Bakelite was the pre-plastic wonder material that ultimately spawned a myriad of high-tech plastics. Old rods made from tapered sticks and bamboo are certainly now relics of a bygone era. Fibreglass and carbon fibre now leading the forefront in fishing technology. At over $600 for a reel alone, the tuna chasers, who seem to congregate in the waters of south western Victoria are well removed from the more simple days of dropping a line off the end of a jetty. One recent long weekend at Portland saw over 300 amateur fishing boats vying for the blue fin tuna. Locals mentioned that the huge influx of boats and fishermen had exhausted the Portland's fuel supplies. Reelin' in the tuna – hey!

Fishing reels and cray measure At Flinders Island.

Old fishing reel from Point King, Portsea, Victoria.

Islands

R emote and distant, difficult access, hidden and obscure, these blobs of terra firma represent a real wilderness for many. Many people living north of Bass Strait have little knowledge of Bass Strait Islands, despite the fact King and Flinders Islands are featured on our nightly Melbourne television weather reports. Out with your Google Earth and have a 'look-see'. Islands have a semi-magical quality. Aloof and distant, most only accessible by sea, (the larger islands like King Island, Flinders Island and Cape Barren Island all have their own runways and airfields.) Interestingly enough, Craggy Island, some 10 kilometres northwest of Flinders Island, has its own helipad, situated on the top of the ridge, in a seemingly precarious position. Craggy has an automated navigational beacon and the helipad is used for servicing this light. Philip Island is one of the few islands with its own road bridge.

The big island is 'Tassie.' Initially called Van Diemans Land and was sighted by Dutchman, Abel Tasman at 4 o'clock in the afternoon, on 24th November, 1642. The name change to 'Tasmania' occurred in 1856. I have always considered Abel Tasman's exploratory voyage a phenomenal effort.

Digger Island, near Walkerville South, Victoria.

Rodondo Island from Wilsons Promontory, Victoria.

With no 'sat. nav.', no radios, no navigational charts, no gyro compasses, not even a reliable chronometer, this is simply an astounding feat to navigate a vessel so far south from known trade routes. I thought I had undertaken a big voyage when I first took my boat down the east coast of Wilson's Promontory, Victoria, and when I crossed the deepest part of Bass Strait, Sisters Passage, to reach Inner Sister Island. How such insignificant obstacles lie before most of us today in our comfortable 21st century world. Only the likes of Jessica Watson and Jesse Martin can claim to have taken on challenges of a gargantuan nature.

Travelling to islands within Australia can be expensive despite air travel becoming relatively inexpensive in recent times. Getting to Tasmania is cheap enough with a $79 fare. But try flying into King or Flinders Island on a commercial plane. Start at around $350. This is precisely why these islands will never be overrun with visitors and holiday makers. You can now fly to Japan one way or even New Zealand far more cheaply than spending hundreds of dollars required to fly out to these Bass Strait islands . But once you are there, on these islands, you immediately step into a time warp. There is a slower and more relaxed pace of life. Friendly locals, drivers who wave to other drivers, the cars are left unlocked and only very recently local island police at Flinders Island began remonstrating with motorists not to leave car keys in the car ignition. The simple life indeed. French Island despite its relative closeness to civilazation, also offers a "time warped" experience.

When you travel in a boat to a smaller island there is an even bigger adventure. The island may not have been visited for months. Perhaps it has been untouched for over a year. What bounty awaits? There may be flotsam and jetsam of all types to discover. There is the wildlife, particularly seabirds, nesting and breeding in the spring. While most of humanity rumbles about its' metropolises, here you are at one with the elements, with nature, with the vagaries of the weather and with time. Take in the scenery, the ocean, the

Embarking for Roydon Island, Eastern Bass Strait.

Roydon Island, my favourite in the
Furneaux Group, Tasmania.

coastline: little else can compare with this experience. This style of 'getaway' is not advertised, nor promoted in your mass-medicated, holiday travel magazines and programs. Hooray. You have freedom at last.

Griffiths Island, at Port Fairy, is probably the most accessible and 'unusual' island in this region. Complete with its' own picturesque lighthouse of traditional construction and built in 1859. Access is via a well constructed concrete causeway which takes pedestrian traffic. The causeway runs along-side the Moyne River. Griffiths Island is a nesting ground for the Shearwaters, these well-travelled birds coming to roost from November to April, having traversed the Pacific Ocean from the Aleutian Island near Alaska!

The most remote and inaccessible island, the island full of mystique and sheer impressiveness is Rodondo Island, 11 kilometres south of Wilsons Promontory. First accessed in 1947 by a group from Scotch College,

Melbourne, it has seldom been visited since. Many sheer cliffs abound on this pyramid-shaped monster, the island soaring to 350 metres. Home to an estimated 1.1 million shearwaters or 'mutton birds', this reserve is simply spectacular. Sometimes partially covered with lenticular cloud, the best viewing position for Rodondo Island has to be from the comfort of the light keepers cottages at Southeast Point Wilsons Promontory. Make the 19 kilometre trek to the lighthouse at Southeast Point, stay two nights at the light keepers residences and not only watch the endless procession of shipping pass by but also the ever-changing kaleidoscope of weather in Bass Strait. Interestingly too, the vegetation on Rodondo Island is similar to that found in Western Australia.

Lady Julia Percy Island near Portland is a basaltic outcrop, at distance rather inhospitable and remote. Less so Rosyth Island in the Furneaux Group. With sandy beaches and idyllic turquoise waters all looks complete. Only locals can attest to the resident mosquito population which rivals French Island (the only place I've seen mosquitos in a swarm.) Select your island carefully before any intended visit. Some offshore islands require permits from the relevant authorities if a visit is contemplated.

Jetties and Piers

Something deep within the human psyche makes us all venture on to these platforms which reach out into the depths of the ocean, where fish and boats, waves and the unknown of the deep are all thrust before us in the most candid and stark nature. Everyone has an exploratory streak and this is best seen by the numbers of people who venture to the end of the planks, or in the case at Lorne, Victoria, the far less romantic concrete construction. Jetties and piers have a history. How else to board a vessel with a deep draft, on any tide, unless we can berth close alongside these utilitarian structures, knowing there is ample water underneath the keel.

As with the history of human civilisation jetties and piers have their own.

The recently reconstructed Naracoopa Jetty on King Island was not only a victory for locals but the restoration work has also preserved an iconic part of the east coast of KI. The working jetty at Port Campbell, with its highly unusual lifting crane ensures commercial fishing boats can gain entry and exit to adjacent fishing grounds quickly, when sea conditions are suitable, by being hoisted into the water and gaining access to the coastline adjacent to the Port Campbell National Park and the iconic Twelve Apostles. The

Fergusons Jetty, Fotheringate Bay, Flinders Island, Tasmania.

Sea wall Point Roadknight, Victoria.

Outstanding Lillies Bay Flinders Island, Tasmania.

Rye Jetty and sailing ship, Victoria.

coastline here being so sheer and dangerous that even in more recent times highly experienced skippers, kayakers and even one of the crew from the local surf lifesaving club had all sadly met their demise after having taken on the challenge of powerful Southern Ocean swell. Please take extreme care when on any exposed coastline.

From Portsea pier, which is presently experiencing more than its share of the heavy ocean swell well within the confines of the usually sheltered Port Phillip Bay, to the long jetty at Beach Port South Australia, which seems to extend almost a kilometre out into the bay. All these structures require continual maintenance. They always have a contingent of amateur fishermen as well as the professionals but increasingly too, visitors and tourists are keen to experience all that these structures have to offer.

Move away from the working jetties, those of recent construction and perhaps even made of concrete ... ah, Lorne Jetty has much to be improved upon, yet is strong and functional. And look for the isolated pylons, the ruins, the history, signs of a bygone era that hark back to days of sail and steam. A few derelict poles are all that remain of the former limestone industry's link with the sea at Digger Island, in south Gippsland. This area was a hive of activity over 100 years ago, but now time and tide have been. Digger Island is reputed to harbour trilobite fossils and is accessible by foot at low tides, being situated just over a kilometre from Walkerville South.

The most forlorn, isolated and sad remnants of any jetty are to be found on Fotheringate Bay, some 8 kilometres south of Whitemark, Flinders Island. Check it out on Google Earth. Absolutely isolated, with no road access, here is a statement to mankind's attempts to 'control nature'. Not only was the jetty built in a very exposed location but the shallow approaches also contributed to its early demise. The remaining timbers thrust 4 to 6 metres into the air and in their own way still act in open defiance to the very elements that will ultimately cause its demise.

A tragic outcome at a Port Phillip Bay pier recently involved a dare with 'mates,' alcohol and a water temperature of 16C, an asthmatic who was a poor swimmer and night time conditions. The picture is clear in dealing with sea. Do not take unnecessary risks at any time. Know your capabilities and act accordingly.

Law of the Sea

Over the years beachcombers will recover numerous items from the shoreline. In Victorian, Tasmanian and South Australian coastlines items the author has found have included wetsuits and diving gear, a surfboard, divers' torches, driftwood, milk crates and fish bins as well as a useable LPG gas cylinder. Who owns these items and what does the law have to say about possession.

Firstly, if any items of shipwreck, especially historical shipwreck, are found then the Commonwealth authorities must be notified. An offence is committed if one retains possession of such items.

Civil law concerns itself with rights to possession. Other found items, like diving gear and surfboards which have been found and are now in your hands mean you have a right to possession which you can legally enforce against all but the true owners. The beachcomber becomes the defacto owner because they have been irretrievably lost by the former owners.

The gas cylinder, fish bins and milk crates present different issues. Because the owners can be identified by the names on the items, people 'collecting' such items may break the law, specifically section 72 and 73 of the Victorian

Milk crate washed ashore, near Gunnamatta, Victoria.

tasmaid

WARNING
THE OWNER WILL PROSECUTE
FOR WITHHOLDING RETURN OR
UNAUTHORIZED USE OF THIS
CONTAINER.

'WARNING Owner will Prosecute'. Milk Crate.

Wetsuit found at Matha Point, Port Phillip Bay, Victoria.

Crimes Act 1958. (Other state legislation would be similar in content.) The best policy is to hand such items into the police and fill out an ownership claim form. If the police return the item to you because the true owner can't be found and no government agency wants the item, then you can keep the item with a clear conscience.

Milk crates present an interesting issue. Over one million of them go 'missing' every year. Some of the crates I have retrieved have been badly damaged when washed up on the rocks or badly scuffed on the sand. I make the judgement that they are not useable and would not be sought after by the owners. This may be a poor assessment on my part, however, and caution would dictate that finders should still attempt to contact the true owners. Possibly a better solution may be to have a deposit on each crate and a finders fee, like the 10 cent refund on drink bottles currently in operation in South Australia.

Lifebuoys

How silly people can be! Especially in the light of the sinking of the Costa Concordia and the 100 year anniversary of the sinking of the Titanic. One would think that marine safety should be on everyone's mind. Who would be silly enough to throw a working lifebuoy overboard? My first find obviously came from the Spirit of Tasmania, Devonport. Only to be recovered on Inner Sister Island, in the Furneaux Group, much the worse for wear, this life buoy was washed up high and dry on the rocky coastline. It had ended up many kilometres due east of the track of the popular interstate ferries, Spirit of Tasmania I and Spirit of Tasmania II. The same held true for life buoys at Rye Pier. Yes good fun to throw them 'overboard' until they are really needed in an emergency.

Rock fishermen along the Great Ocean Road in Victoria, now have available serviceable life buoys at strategic locations. Let's hope they are never used. Sadly, twenty two rock fishermen lost their lives in New South Wales in a 24 month period in recent years. The message is crystal clear. Take extreme care when venturing near the sea and don't abuse lifesaving equipment. The more traditional looking life buoy with its red bands and white vinyl covering

Life buoy located on Inner Sister Island Tasmania.

SWITCH OFF
MOBILE PHONES

Mobile phone sign recovered from Limestone Bay Bass Strait.

Emergency life line Middle Pascoe Island,
Furneaux Group, Tasmania.

is probably the poorest when it comes to 'saving life'. As the Tamar Marine (Launceston) catalogue indicates: 'not approved (by marine authorities) but ideal for boat or pool.' By comparison, the heavy duty life buoy, SOLAS approved, 30" with rigid foam, would certainly give a drowning person a headache if he or she were to be thrown this buoy and got a hit on the head for their troubles. If you intend doing any serious coastal forays why not invest in a light-weight, self-inflating PFD yolk, which can be worn under your clothes? At under $100 they make for an excellent investment.

Lighthouses

The power, the allurement, the history and the iconic nature of these structures are well known to all who venture near our fantastic coastline. The lifesaving capabilities of our standout navigational aids have no fancy black box electronics. Pure masonry and construction. Almost foolproof illumination. Let them 'stand' for a thousand years.

Short or narrow, stumpy and squat. Older and intricate, concrete masonry and little imagination. Majestic and overpowering. Lighthouses come in all shapes and sizes. They come in all manner of design. The most appealing ones are the older structures. When time was less precious and lighthouses were an essential element of infrastructure for our fledgling nation. With 400 souls perishing on an early August night in 1845, the inbound Cataraqui became our largest maritime disaster. The tragedy occurred metres from the King Island coastline. Ultimately, this horrific disaster resulted in the construction of Australia's tallest lighthouse at Cape Wickham, on possibly Australia's flattest island, King Island.

Today we can swiftly drive to their doorsteps. We can even stay at the lightkeepers' cottages: Cape Otway, Wilsons Promontory and Point Hicks

Cape Schanck Lighthouse, Victoria.

Currie Light at King Island.

just to name a few. The Cape Martin light, situated near the South Australian town of Beachport, was a 'have to visit' for our family. Is your lighthouse awaiting a visit? The most magic of all locations is Southeast Point, Wilsons Promontory. Do take the 19 kilometre trek, stay for two nights, ensuring a rest and exploratory day. Watch the ships pass by in procession. Gaze upon the remote and solitary Rodondo Island, part of Tasmania, and peer into the Bass Strait haze to the southeast and Hogan Island and the Kent Group.

The Eastern Lighthouse at McCrae (Mornington Peninsula, Victoria) and the lighthouse at Currie, King Island, Tasmania) are almost identical in design. Metallic in construction, they are unusual in their fabrication. The Currie light is open for tours. The internal spiral staircase is a statement in design and symmetry. The nearby former keepers cottage is now used as a very interesting museum.

And while you're out and about at Currie, on 'K. I', as the locals refer to King Island, the Cape Wickham lighthouse is a must see. Soaring to over 70 metres, this is the tallest lighthouse in Australia. (Google Map -39.588526, 143.943066) However, the highest lighthouse is at the eastern end of Bass Strait on Deal Island. At around 300 metres in elevation, this lighthouse can be shrouded in cloud. It has now been decommissioned for a number of years and a lower light 'beacon' is now situated at Erith Island, part of the Kent Group. If you can't make it out to Deal Island, you may get a glimpse of the Deal 'lighthouse' when flying between Flinders Island and Victoria. Interestingly, there is a long waiting list of volunteers who wish to spend a stint out at Deal, one of the last wilderness areas in this part of the world. Of the earliest lighthouses in Australia, six were built in Tasmania, including the Deal Island lighthouse. (Google Map 39.49404,147.316915).

Aireys Inlet lighthouse was featured in the well-known children's program which ran for a number of years: 'Around the Twist'. If travellers only visited the many lighthouses along the coastline in our part of the world they would

McCrae Lighthouse, Victoria.

Wilsons Promontory light at sunset, Victoria.

be never disappointed. But do take the time to take a tour, be it Cape Schanck, Aireys Inlet or Swan Island, a more remote island off the north eastern coast of Tasmania.

But why do lighthouses have such an attraction ? Sharma Krauskopf, Scottish lighthouse owner and author of a tantalizing book on 'Scottish Lighthouses' sums it up this way. Lighthouses are almost invariably in remote locations, perhaps there is an associated 'wilderness experience. Lighthouses all have a very close relationship with the sea. Because of their seaborne localities, lighthouses can be excellent viewing platforms for marine creatures as well as migratory and shorebirds. Lighthouses are also a part of our history. And the physical beauty of these structures is, as well, one of the great attractions, so much so that many of these buildings appear on the National Heritage register. Krauskopf closes her 'intellectual reasons' for lighthouses with an emotional moment to which we can all relate. The description is simply a dark night and the piercing, rotating, beam of light radiating into the blackness. The only thought to add is that the 'pulse' or heartbeat of the lighthouse, the beam, is almost an inviolable part of its being. They are ultimately dependable, reliable and unchanging in a very dynamic and otherwise fast-paced world. Interestingly, Scotland was the first country in the world to organize lighthouse construction and management through the government.

Do yourself a favour. Plan to stay in at least one light keepers cottage around our massive coastline. If you want to see four lighthouses at the one time, a visit to Point Nepean on the southern Mornington Peninsula is a must. Good visibility is required to pick up the Cape Schank lighthouse but the Point Lonsdale lighthouse and the Queenscliff lighthouses are all within easy viewing distance. Queenscliff has a White lighthouse and a Black lighthouse, the black masonry being the volcanic rock, basalt, which is commonly referred to as 'Bluestone'. Apparently this is the only 'black' structure of its type in the southern hemisphere.

View from Cape Otway Lighthouse, Victoria.

Mystery of the Whale Skull

Some of the most powerful coastline to be found in Bass Strait, apart from the Shipwreck Coast and the Twelve Apostles, can be found between Cape Franklin and Twelve Hour Point, Flinders Island. Huge boulders, only ever moved in the most powerful of seas, rising granitic cliffs,

Mystery whale skull seen near Cape Franklin, Flinders Island.

wind scoured headlands, perhaps the solitary flight of a sea eagle and a rough 4WD track that bent our suspension. This is tough, rough, and challenging country. If the Australian outback is true wilderness then this is coastal wilderness.

Many years have now past since my first visit here. The first time I saw this object I had no idea what it was. Grey, bulbous, high and dry on the berm at the highest point of the rock strewn coastline there was this 'object.' At around two metres in circumference it was massive, whatever it was. After visiting a number of whale locations around the coast of Flinders Island and the very informative local museum, I reckoned that the object was a whale skull. Perhaps from a blue whale. Some years later I returned to this location. Nothing was to be seen of this skull. Sadly I have no photographs to reinforce my tale. Can anyone help?

Naval Flares

Once upon a beachcombing day, the sun was shining, the wind was gently blowing, all was well until, as chance would have it, there lay an aluminium cylinder with a partially obliterated but still legible warning sign: Danger: Marine Flare. Notify Police, etc. Being at a remote area it took a few hours to walk out and get back to civilisation and a phone, whereby the police were duly notified.

Within a few days, a chartered plane flew out from Hobart, complete with a Defence Forces bomb disposal expert. When a local police officer and the miliary personal had driven up from the airport we drove out to the coast to find the location of this 'ordinance'. After hiking back along the coastline we found the device and the disposals expert went about setting a charge of plastic explosive to detonate the naval flare. Surprisingly the whole act played out very quickly and with a small bang and a puff of smoke, the explosion rendered the flare inactive. I later learned that naval operations had taken place in the Great Australian Bight and a small number of these flares had proven defective. Some flares had already been located along the south eastern Australian coastline. One particular flare was duly loaded into a utility where

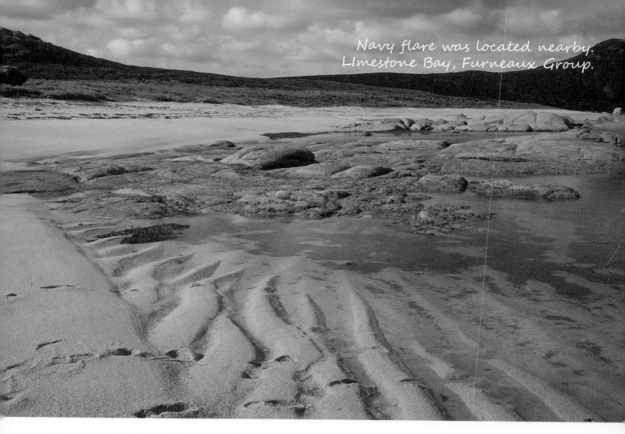

it eventually ignited and set fire to the vehicle. If there are any lessons to be learned by beachcombers, one in particular would be to take care when 'UFO's are found. The 'unidentified flammable objects' may include all types of chemicals in drums and containers, fuel and other caustic materials which could certainly cause injury to the unwary and unsuspecting beachcomber.

The Bondi Rescue featured in a similar incident and in this case the beach was cordoned off for a radius of 300 metres prior to the Defence Force personnel deactivating the device. Trawling the web for marine or military flares shows that this type of occurrence is not uncommon. From Canada to the USA, Hawaii and the UK these potentially dangerous devices do wash up on beaches from time to time. The biggest danger may be that children can find these items. The phosphorus burns at 1650C and some flares contain a detonator!

If you find a flare phone 000 immediately.

Navigation Lights and Instruments

Anything nautical, especially old or new, will appeal to diehard collectors. Old navigation lights can be sourced from boatyards as they set about upgrading and replacing corroded units. But an exploratory dive can also locate some rubbish that has been inappropriately jettisoned. My favourite marine light, now in service again as an emergency shack light when the power goes down, was recovered off the Blairgowrie Yacht Squadron Marina. Similarly at Portsea, a mast light, fallen prey to the elements, was spotted on the sea floor during one of our weekly swims. This again is rewired and now has another life as an emergency camping light. Disused gauges come in any number of shapes and varieties. The trim tab meters and an old diving depth gauge both have their own appeal, if not just for their analogue dials but that they now represent maritime history.

Compass housing donated by R. Purdon, Tasmania.

Emergency light found on South Pascoe Island Tasmania.

Full speed ahead, Glenelg, Adelaide.

Navigation light in shack found at
Blairgowrie yacht moorings, Victoria.

Nets

Mostly found objects, the various types and grades of nets come in an assortment of weave patterns, thicknesses and colours.

From the delicate seine nets to heavy duty trawl fishery nets that can handle tonnes of weight, there is a richness of diversity that makes for an interesting study.

Nets, old and used, have numerous non-marine uses including covers for vegetable patches where birds are a problem. We used our nets as trellises to encourage vines and creeper growth at our windswept campsite. Another of our net finds was wrapped around our water tank to encourage creepers and passionfruit vines. Yet other nets where used on post and wire fences to stop dogs and foxes getting into our backyard.

Net floats are another aspect to beachcombing. An interesting assortment of shapes, colours and materials can be made from a collection of these smaller but essential pieces of fishing gear. From traditional cork to the various types of styrofoam and marine grade plastic, net floats are attached to the nets in a variety of ways. Nets are usually repaired in the off-season or when bad weather prevents fishermen from going to sea.

Tangled fishing net, British Admiral Beach, King Island.

Shark net floats washed in from southern Bass Strait.

The poor seal was spotted near Cape Liptrap, Southern Victoria, fouled in some shark netting. It scampered off into the water before we could provide assistance.

Propellers

The bronze and older style props are infinitely preferred to the mass produced alloy outboard props of today. The older style propellers have a certain history and style. If they are recovered from boatwrecks and shipyards so much the better. My favourite, recently acquired from a good friend in Tasmania is the 'kelp cutter.' A two blade setup with minimal style, it appears to be many years old. Little is known of its origins. Props can be garnered from scrap metal merchants, boat repairers and the like.

Nautically themed museums around our coastline have many exhibits from the ships that foundered on these shores. From the recently upgraded and renovated Furneaux Museum at Flinders Island to the Low Head Pilot Station Maritime Museum, there's plenty to keep visitors interested and enthused. Propellers I've seen on the beach have either been frozen onto 'prop' shafts on beached vessels or were simply too large to 'salt away' in a backback.

Abandoned prop near Currie wharf, King Island

Salvaged propellers.

Rocks

From the impressive and monolithic Old Mans Head to Cape Woolamai and Pulpit Rock at Cape Schanck, rocks say it all. The 'Australia's Granite Wonderlands', a beautifully presented publication on the granites of Australia has many images of coastal rocks, standout features in a standout continent, Australia. Granites, in particular, can be found throughout the region but other rock types, from sedimentary sandstones to volcanic basalt also abound in the area. A special place for rock hopping, rock study and rock specimen collection can be found between Cape Liptrap and Walkerville, in South Gippsland. This area has been described as one of the most geologically significant areas along the entire Victorian coastline. The difficult terrain encountered here ensures minimal foot traffic. Very low tides and low swell are essential for intrepid coastal walkers. In this area are found greenstone, folded sedimentary layers, black sands or rutile and much more. The limestone stacks at Grinder Point are a special feature.

Cleft Rock or Skull Rock off Wilsons Promontory is far less accessible than Castle Rock, on the west coast of Flinders Island. Both are very deserving of 'spectacular' status in the 'best rock' stakes. Castle Rock has featured on front

Lichen covered boulders Tasmania.

covers and in articles on Flinders Island. This rock was also the subject of an image that won the Australian 'landscape photograph' of the year.

With coastal weathering being a major feature of our environment there are many exposed rocks to be seen. The most colourful rocks may be found at the 'coloured cliffs' between Peterborough and Childers Cove in South Western Victoria. A stunning location that matches the swath of colours on a landscape artists' palette.

Lichen coloured rocks are another special feature in parts of Bass Strait and its entrances. From the picturesque Broken Arm Beach at King Island to the rock strewn coastline around Wilsons Promontory there is much to leave

Lone Apostle Port Campbell National Park, Victoria.

Seal on the rocks, Cape Patton,
Great Ocean Road, Victoria.

The most famous of all rocks. Twelve Apostles, Victoria.

us inspired. The 'calcified forests' are another unusual feature to investigate. They can be found from Victoria's Cape Bridgewater to the Mornington Peninsula and on the Bass Strait Islands of Flinders and King Island.

Isolated rocks like the seal colony at Tasmania's Wrights Rock and Victoria's Higginbotham Rocks both have their claims to fame. Get out and see some of this fabulous coastal geomorphology before it's too late. Stop Press: One of the Twelve Apostles collapsed 26th September 2009. How long before new apostles 'arise' or another one topples? Ours is a dynamic coast.

Ropes

Simple yet essential, ropes have figured as vital shipping gear for thousands of years. What has happened in recent times is the proliferation of nylon and polypropylene rope, far more durable than the hemp and sisal ropes of yesteryear. Today, the fishing industry in particular still relies on ropes. Be it for trawl nets, long-line and shark or cray fishing. Ropes are the literal life-line for this multi-million dollar industry. Hawser ropes for domestic and international cargo ships are the heavy duty big boys of the maritime industry.

If you find a tangled mess of rope on some desolate shore, expect to spend the best part of 20 to 30 minutes to untangle the mess. It's very therapeutic. If you're lucky, your rope will reveal an assortment of stainless steel clips and a buoy or two.

One aspect deserves attention. Experienced deck-hands and marine collectors will instantly feel the smoothness or roughness of the rope at first grab. The newer rope materials, as well as some more traditional ropes, are definitely not as user-friendly as the silky smooth ropes

Rope with the greatest longevity still used for free diving as a towline

Ships hawser at Narrawong,
near Portland, Victoria.

Coiled rope shower base, Koh Samui, Thailand.

between my catch bag and float, was recovered on a coastal walk between Mallacoota and Nadgee Nature Reserve, N.S.W. The remote coastline at Cape Howe, on the N.S.W. and Victorian border, has less visitors than Cape York, at the tip of far North Queensland. One important tip for the avid rope beach collector is to rinse your find in fresh water prior to use. Our 100mm garden rope, complete with white posts, finally succumbed to elements after a number of years. I figured that a pre-soak and rinse may have extended its shelf-life considerably.

At days end, where ever you hang your hat and your beachcombing booty, rope knots and rope work are a sure-fire way to keep you in the know. Grab a book on knots or visit a website. Sheep shank, reef, bowline and a score more knots will fire your curiosity. Try your hand at splicing after you have fashioned a fid out of any suitable material available. Yachties and boaties should have no need to bother.

Sea Elephant Tusk

O ne of my most treasured finds – easily as good as a whale's tooth and probably rarer.

A slow trek along a sandy beach at king tide to visit one of my favourite dive locations was richly rewarded with more than cuttlebone, which was my first thought when I saw this 'object' at some distance. Probably the result of a stranding of a sea elephant many years ago, Palana Beach and Blyth Bay, Flinders Island, have been the site for a number of strandings of large marine creatures over the years. A visit to the Emita Museum, on Flinders Island, and a search of the whale photographic albums will reward the patient researcher with numerous instances of similar strandings which have occurred here. It is interesting to consider research findings done on Sea Elephant Bay, King Island where historical records were used to estimate the elephant population at around 13000 in the early days of white settlement, prior to their extermination by 'sealers' and 'whalers.' Using Google Maps on your smart phone or PC, type in 'Blyth Bay, Flinders Island' to hone in on a superb part of Bass Strait.

Sea Elephant Tusk

Location: Palana Beach, Flinders Island, Tasmania

Google Map: 39.761311, 147.883737

Date: January 1980's

Features: Measuring 140mm by 45mm at its widest point, there is an ivory-like tip which is just noticeable at the top of this image

Sea Shells, Abalones and Paper Nautilus

We all have a 'couple' of mementos from a visit to a favourite beach. I blame my parents for dragging me, kicking and screaming, to Queenscliff and Torquay when I was but a babe-in-arms. Grandparents played a roll in my seashell addiction with their large conch shell and the painted fan shells in the sunroom of their Melbourne home, one couldn't help but be impressed and envious. Later, my neighbours took me to Safety beach and Dromana to swim and dive, and collect more shells. A beach always has shells and they become permanent reminders of our excursions to these hallowed precincts.

Conchology is the study of seashells and conchologists are the serious collectors of these beach souvenirs. Cowries hold a fascination with beach goers. We had a great Xmas one year at Green Island scouring the sandy lee shore to collect scores of these sought-after 'gems.' The serious collectors might aim to fill a jar of cowries over many years of collecting. There are the distinctive zig-zag patterned volutes found from Wilsons Promontory to Portsea and beyond. Super large limpet shells, up to 75mm across at the

Shell collection from Victoria, Tasmania and South Australia.

Mounted abalone shells.

base, are becoming a more difficult find. Live Limpets are now protected in
Tasmanian waters. And don't forget the 'no take' zone in Victorian waters
to two metres below the low water mark. Razor Shells seem to be a rare but
prized find. Rarer and treasured 'specimens' were the fossilized shells from a
Tasmanian coastal bushwalking trek. And to display your treasures, a sea shell
table is obligatory. Go seek your sea shell upon the sea shore. Mitre shells, the
prized murex, cones and auger shells and the 'Chinese fingernails' are all part
of the vast and varied array of these marine molluscs.

Abalone shells are usually the biggest shell on any beach, and they gain
our attention not only for their sheer size but also because of their attractive
mother of pearl colouring. Early settlers called this mollusc 'mutton fish'.
Later, the humble abalone spawned a multi-million dollar seafood industry
within Australia and globally. In other parts of the world this mother of pearl

is a sought after material for souvenir manufacturers. I've always liked the smaller shells because of their delicate nature and also because the colours can be more subtle. One of my first introductions to the commercial world of 'ab' diving was meeting two professional abalone divers at Fingal Beach, Cape Schanck on the central coastline of Victoria a number of years ago. They had each made about $600 for the day by commercially free diving. When we investigated the license costs, which were pushing up to $1 million in those days we decided to keep our day jobs. That wasn't before a neighbour and myself had approached the National Australia Bank and had also completed the necessary diving medicals. Dream on.

Back in the real world, diving recreationally for green lip abalone in Tasmania I have enjoyed many a stir fry with this exorbitantly priced seafood. While a recreational fishing licence in Tasmania costs around $60 per annum this is small change alongside the abalone which can be found for sale at Tullamarine airport, Melbourne, where prices push well over $200 per kilogram. These greenlip abalone are an amazing creature. Not only is the very tough abalone shell being studied at the molecular level for its exceptional strength, apparently because the microscopic calcium carbonate is stacked like bricks and may lead to improved body armour for defence force personal, but also of note is the amazing adhesive strength of the foot of these green lipped 'beasts'. I have yet to break a diving knife prising off a large green lip that may be over 150 mm at the widest point. But when these abalone are taken from a granite rock small particles of that rock will be imbedded in the foot. Obviously you will find green lips in some of the most exposed ocean locations as strong ocean swell and current is little deterrent to their mobility. The taste and look of the 'greens' far exceeds those of the blacklip variety. In Tasmania the bag limit for licensed divers is 10 per day making it possible to gather sufficient of these sought after molluscs for a big feast. Just add onion, fry quickly after preparation and enjoy.

Black lip abalone pale into comparison compared with the flesh of the green lips. Shell collectors will notice a difference between the two varieties. The abalones are valued by many Asian countries for their medicinal properties.

Probably the saddest chapter in the life of abalone in recent years is the outbreak of the viral disease ganglioneuritis in Victoria and New South Wales. Hopefully Tasmania, which produces up to 25% of the world abalone harvest will remain disease-free with stringent fishing regulations currently in force to stop the spread of this devastating disease.

Paper Nautilus shells are so unusual that my first shell find at Flinders ocean beach, south of Melbourne, left me in a quandary. Was it some ornate Japanese artefact washed off a ship? Did the shell originate from the creative workshops of artisans in Asia? My biology colleague was quick to come to my aid. 'Where did you find that?' he said. ' I've always wanted to find a nautilus shell but never had any luck.' So started my fascination with the paper nautilus shell.

Spending many autumn seasons on the magical Flinders Island, Tasmania, our family came to be well placed for the expected seven year cycle, which locals maintain, sees these unique shells washed up on beaches around the island in eastern Bass Strait. The tide has to be falling, the weather calm and the advice was to get there early, preferably predawn.

As we camped one year during the autumn, we noticed an unusual amount of early morning traffic, at around 0300 hours, on an otherwise deserted road. Not that the locals would tell us anything. Shell collecting is serious business in Bass Strait. In the earlier days of shell collecting prices of up to $10 per shell could be procured. Was it any wonder that local fishermen and residents would be up well before dawn scouring the beaches and coastline on the western side of the island to make their fortunes. One local on Flinders Island was reported to have been aiming to collect one thousand shells which would be slowly sold off over the coming years and when there was the inevitable drought of shell strandings. The keen collectors use trail bikes and quad bikes and rise in the very early morning hours to hit the beaches well before dawn.

As the sun rises and the stranded Argonauts and their shells litter the beaches, shorebirds and particularly the silver gulls pick a neat hole in the side of the shell for a good feed.

Interestingly the delicate nautilus shell is the egg case of an octopus Argonauta Nodosa. This is the female shell, the male nautilus very small.

So at 3:30 a.m. one cold autumn night our family set out on West End beach with gas lantern in hand ready for the big haul of Nautilus shells. We collected 45 to 50 shells which was a mammoth effort for visitors from the mainland. Residents at Palana, Flinders Island, were very surprised to see us returning to our vehicle on first light. But as local knowledge is always better with such things, the pair walked to Bun Beetons Point where there was another hidden sandy cove and they bagged 90 shells if my memory serves me correctly. Still, our family was ecstatic with our find. I have heard that some of the rare specimen shells have ended up as far away as New York as well as Western Australia. They are currently priced at around $25 per shell. I can see that over time collectors who take shells for commercial gain will have to be licensed. This might put them in conflict with amateur collectors. Perhaps it would be better to maintain the present law of the sea and the beach: finders keepers. The legal rights of beachcombers and their booty is dealt with elsewhere.

Living close to the sea and swimming weekly can also have its advantages. A group of my friends take a weekly splash into the briny at Portsea jetty on the southern Mornington Peninsula, located at the southern end of Port Phillip Bay, Victoria. One winter's afternoon in August, about three years ago, with water temperature around 12°, a good swimming buddy and I set off on the 40 to 50 minute swim along the shores of Weeroona Bay. There had been, prior to our swim, the occasional sighting of a lone nautilus shell here and there. My diving buddy and I hit the jackpot. Swimming slowly along the shoreline in under two metres of water, heading towards Point Nepean National Park. We both collected a dozen large, fine specimen shells, resting on the sea floor,

King Island limpets display.

One thousand shells, Shelly Beach, via Portland, Victoria.

where the gentle turbulence of the backwash from the small waves hitting the beach, had appeared to neatly deposit these delicate treasures of the sea. Every year we still look for the shells during the cooler months, but these Nautilus strandings are fickle in nature and literally unpredictable. Perhaps chaos theory has a place here.

Another place to look for shells, albeit very small ones, is surprisingly, around the mouth of creeks abutting Port Phillip Bay. One such creek is Chinaman's Creek, at Rosebud. I was somewhat amazed to go for a lunchtime walk past the creek and pick up a couple of these very small Paper Nautilus shells, partially hidden by the seaweed. Fresh footprints indicated people had been walking on the beach but unless you look carefully and you know what to look for you may miss the mark. I've found something similar when I've been with inexperienced divers looking for abalone. Again, knowing what to look for and taking your time can pay good dividends.

Professor Edward Greding wrote a thought provoking article entitled: 'Journey Deep in Time'. He highlights that paleontological evidence clearly indicates the slowing of the earth and the moon's rotation. He used fossilized Nautilus shells as his evidence. As a nautilus grows within its shell it secretes a new chamber into which it moves. The old chamber is sealed off with a septum. Today we find an average of 30 fine lamentations which appears to indicate that each combination represents one day and the whole process is tied to the 30 day lunar cycle. Fossil nautilus shells over 400 million years ago show only nine or 10 lamentations which indicates the lunar cycle at this time must have been only nine or 10 days. Astronomers can calculate past orbital periods and distances for the earth-moon system and it is amazing to consider that our moon may have been a mere 160,000 kilometres away, doubtless a very impressive sight and about 40% of its present distance. The earth day would have been 21 hours long and each year would have been 417 days. Long live the nautilus.

Shacks and Boat Sheds

Truly iconic features of the Australian beachscape, be it the brightly coloured, passive bayside boat sheds or the more traditional 'pioneer' and utilitarian abodes, these shacks and boat sheds are now recognized at all levels of government. They are rated and regulated. They are even enshrined in Tasmanian legislation which, in recent years, granted freehold title to scores of owners who had built their pieces of paradise on Crown land. The official position now goes along the lines of 'shacks contributing to cultural, historical and recreational' aspects of our lives. Nowadays all dwellings must conform to uniform building regulations. Shacks and boat sheds go way back to a time when fishermen, holiday campers and even those down on their luck fashioned a shelter out of whatever materials were available. Perhaps as a derivative of our bushranging heritage and perhaps also because many Australians' forebears were criminals, lawbreakers and convicts, people today will use their shacks and boat sheds illegally, to live and habitate over the summer months. As the author of a book on Australian shacks recently quoted: it wouldn't be a shack if there wasn't something illegal about it.'

Boat sheds at Tyrone Foreshore, Rye, Victoria.

Boat shed, Rosebud, Port Phillip Bay, Victoria.

Shacks in Bass Strait.

Shack interior.

What I like best about boat sheds and shacks around the coast is the creativity and inventiveness as well as the diversity of these creations. Never built along the lines of your standard two storey mac- mansion, shacks and sheds have allowed generations of Australians to more individualize their own personalities. There are seemingly as many different styles of shacks and boat sheds are there are builders. And as housing becomes more unaffordable, and the talk of the next global financial crisis mounts, a rebirth of shacks may be imminent. Certainly, when bayside boatsheds are selling at well in excess of $100 000 there would appear to be a huge disconnect between the idealism and historical aspects of boatsheds and their lack of affordability for your average beachgoer.

It is interesting to see that a recent episode of Gardening, Australia ABC1, was partly filmed in a Tassy shack near Hobart. Oh yes it was a shed alright, completed with roll-clad lining, bed, kitchen and kitchen sink and all the accruements needed for a comfortable 'holiday abode.' With prices, then, reaching astronomical proportions, take your beach umbrella, chairs and towels and have just as good a time at the beach for a fraction of the cost.

Shipwrecks

From the days of sail, the number of wrecks from the early days of maritime history in our waters beggars belief. There are over 6000 wrecks that we know of, Eastern Australian wrecks perhaps starting with Sydney Cove at Preservation Island, Furneaux Group, Tasmania, but which is preceded by the mythical 'Mahogany Ship' near Warrnambool. All contribute to our rich, heroic and often tragic seafaring history. The greatest disaster was the Cataraqui which struck a reef at King Island in 1845. Around 400 souls perished on a dark August night, claiming the infamy of being Australia's biggest peacetime loss of life in coastal waters. Essential reading for those interested in all things seafaring and nautical, have to be the stories of the demise of the Cataraqui and the Loch Ard, which foundered below the precipitous cliffs near Port Campbell. While there is little to see of the remains of the Cataraqui, save some relics at the local museum at King Island, the famous peacock retrieved from the Loch Ard, almost completely intact from below the perpendicular cliffs of the Port Campbell National Park is an inspirational piece which can be found on display at the Warrnambool Maritime Museum, Warrnambool.

Wreckage from 'Eric the Red' Otway coastline, Victoria.

Paddle Steamer Shannon, 1906 King Island.

Scuttling of the Canberra off Barwon Heads, Victoria.

Fuji anchors on the Shipwreck Coast, Victoria.

Ship anchor, Currie, King Island.

You can dive on the Evian, a former coastal trader, in a few metres of water near Rye pier. The Godfrey is visible at low tide from the lookout along the Great Ocean Road.

The big time wrecks can be found in 70 metres of water off Wilsons Promontory and off Cape Otway. At about 11pm on Thursday November 7, 1940, the Cambridge sank, having collided with a sea mine. One sailor perished but fortunately the other 57 crew were rescued. Similarly the City of Rayville also struck a mine a day later at 7.47pm on the 8 November and suffered an identical demise.

The sailing ship, the William Salthouse, was discovered by scuba divers doing a drift dive within the confines of Port Phillip Bay. The barrels and pork bones can still be seen littering the sea floor. Permits are required to dive at this location.

Perhaps one of the most impressive shipwreck sites, sadly now fallen prey to tide and weather, was the wreck of the City of Foochow, on the east coast of Flinders Island. Driving through farmland and then coastal scrub and fore dunes we were greeted with the sight of an awe-inspiring mast that rose majestically above the dune. We waited in eager anticipation to see the rest of this fine ship. Alas, only the mast remained. A real' wow' factor was here for all who made the effort to come and see the remains of this former coal carrier. The iron mast from the City of Foochow, wrecked in 1877 stayed upright more than 100 years, until 1987, when it finally collapsed. Visit http://www.wrecksite.eu/wreck.aspx?54347 to get a glimpse of the mast.

The scuttling of the HMAS Canberra off Barwon Heads 4th October 2009 had hundreds of onlookers, both seaborne and land based, witness this small piece of history. Increasingly, authorities are making continuing good use of these once proud ships. The Farsund, a Flinders Island wreck that is visible with much of its superstructure still above the water line, recently was the subject of a centenary commemoration.

Shorebirds and Migratory Birds

It is impossible to ignore the prolific birdlife along our shores. The more time devoted to coastal forays the more likely it is that you will encounter any number of shorebirds. Usually there is little danger to the keen bird observer. However, passing by a seagull rookery in a remote part of Bass Strait you maybe dive-bombed by very enthusiastic seagulls. Perhaps flightless young juveniles are laying vulnerably in their nests. It may become prudent to grab a couple of large branches to inhibit the dive- bombing and intimidatory tactics of these birds.

Far less threatening are the Ruddy Turnstones of King Island. Weighing in at around 90 grams, they are least likely to pose any threat to human intervention. What's amazing about the turnstones is their recently discovered migratory habits. They were tagged on King Island only to be identified in Taiwan less than a month later. Similar findings were later confirmed for birds at Flinders, southeast of Melbourne.

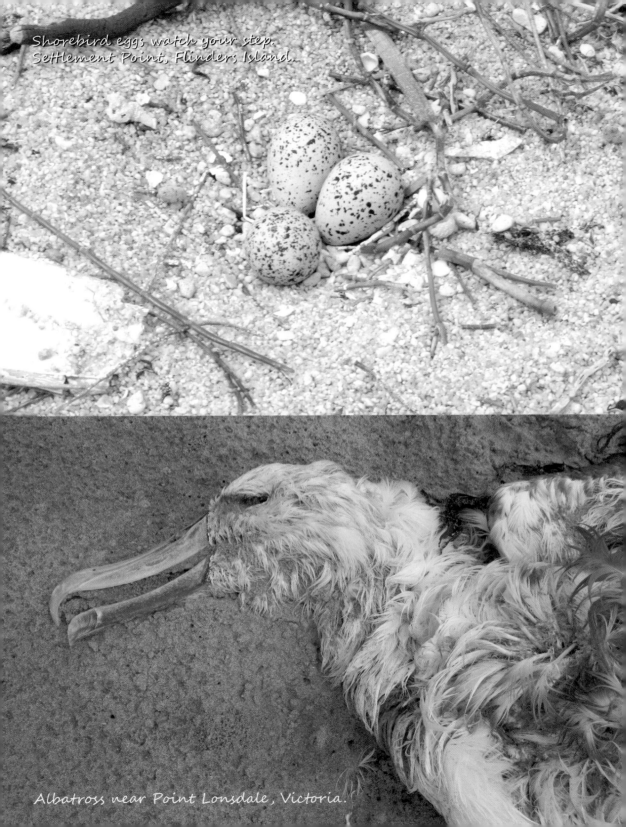

Shorebird eggs watch your step.
Settlement Point, Flinders Island.

Albatross near Point Lonsdale, Victoria.

Pelican beak found on Rye bay beach, Victoria.

Short-tailed Shearwater

Mutton Bird rookery Flinders Island, Tasmania.

Shore Bird habitat,
Gunnamatta, Victoria

Most spectacular of all the seabirds, and my own favourite, is the superb sea eagle. With a wingspan of around two metres, they are impressive from any angle. Usually keeping their distance, I chanced upon a sole sea eagle early one morning, making the most of a dead eel washed up on the high tide. The sea eagle quickly took to flight as I rounded a small headland. They are truly impressive to see at close quarters. Even the more distantly observed birds are a sight to see. With a 25 knot north westerly wind lashing Twelve Hour Point, on the northwest coast of Flinders Island, a solitary sea eagle was soaring in the updrafts, oblivious to human intervention. An awesome sight.

Shearwaters are endemic to this region and Bass Strait is home to many thousands of these birds. They are still seasonally harvested in the Furneaux Group, where they are considered a delicacy. At the recently upgraded Furneaux Museum there is a replica of a mutton-bird processing shed. When early explorers first set sight on this region, shearwater numbers were reckoned at over one million birds. The journal accounts make for stunning reading. Between November and April, before these well-travelled migratory birds set off for the Aleutian Islands near Alaska, many hundreds will be seen at sea, feeding, diving and soaring as they set about the daily business of getting a feed.

Always be on the lookout for any banded birds that come across your path. The author chanced upon a deceased bird along the Mornington Peninsula National Park some years ago. After notifying Parks Victoria of the banding details I was informed this juvenile Gannet, a mere 12 months of age, had flown from New Zealand a month earlier. An amazing feat for such a young bird.

The mighty Albatross is a long revered denizen of the ocean skies. From South America came one such bird, to sadly meet his (or her) demise in a paddock on the northern part of Flinders Island. More recently, a Shy Albatross was identified at Blairgowrie, on the Mornington Peninsula, some 70 kilometres south of Melbourne. This particular bird had been banded two months earlier on Albatross Island, Tasmania. While this specimen was only 16 years old, these birds have been reported to live up to one hundred years.

My most recent 'bird' find, in July of 2013, was a banded, deceased Little Penguin. The penguin was recovered at Killiecrankie Bay, Flinders Island and was initially banded at Phillip Island, Victoria. The time between banding and

recovery is 23 years and 6 months and 20 days, making it the second oldest Little Penguin ever recovered in Australia. This penguin had moved a distance of 275 kilometres. This penguin was banded by the Penguin Study Group and the Australian Bird Banding Scheme has been responsible for maintaining this database.

Squid Jigs

Taking pride of place in our nautical display, these jigs represent hundreds of hours of coastal foraging. Rocky coastlines, remote and inaccessible islands, voyages in boats as well as coastal traversing on foot have finally resulted in this unique collection. The bigger picture is, of course, the squid fishing industry, from which these jigs derive.

A spectacular sight is that of the professional squid boats working out in Bass Strait over the warmer months of the year. I have counted up to thirteen squid boats working way off the surf coast of south western Victoria. These heavily illuminated boats are an unmistakable sight at night. Portland, Queenscliff and Port Fairy are just a few of the seaside towns from which these squid boats operate. The squid industry catch in Victoria during the period 2009/2012 was approximately 70 tonnes, with a value of around $800,000. Squid boats are unmistakable for their many large lights and numerous fishing reels. Go check one out. If you can only look and admire your collection of squid fishing remnants you will find that most of these jigs will glow in the dark after exposure to light. Lights out!

Colourful squid jigs.

Weather

Whether the weather be hot or whether the weather be not, whatever the weather we'll weather the weather, whether we like it or not! So says the 'ye old' English rhyme.

Here is the place to experience all the weathers* that the Southern Ocean and Bass Strait can throw up at us. Intense cold fronts, water spouts, bull nose 'roll clouds', brilliant sunrises and sunsets. Storm force winds are not uncommon in this region. If Borneo and the Malaysian state of Sabah are known as 'the land below the wind' then Bass Strait is right in there! Perhaps the land and ocean here can be named as 'within the wind.'

The 'roaring 40's' pump through Bass Strait and we are relatively close to those 'furious 50's'. Weathering a recent Easter in Bass Strait a cold front and wind up to 74 knots came through, delaying the Three Peaks yachting and running race, capsizing a yacht off Port Campbell and drowning a person in Tasmanian waters. This full-on weather was preceded the previous day by a sea fog that lingered for most of the day in almost dead-calm conditions. On the Beaufort Scale this wind, 74 knots, equates to cyclonic conditions. Hold on to your hat if you can. A boat blew off its trailer near our camp, fencing was

Sunset from Mount Killiecrankie, Flinders Island

Roll Cloud Furneaux Group, Bass Strait, Tasmania.
Image: Bill Hipkiss

Weather near Beachport, South Australia.

down, boats broke from their moorings and it was just another day at the office in Bass Strait. A few years ago our cray pot took some storm force weather. The top part of the pot was located nearly 4 kilometres down the coast after the storm abated.

The stunning location known as Old Man's Head on the northern part of Flinders Island is another place to witness the fury of nature. From dead calm, with a brewing and evil looking sky, within 30 minutes this headland can be transformed into a maelstrom of fury and anger. Whitecaps as far as the eye can see. Here we make increasing use of the Bureau of Meteorology forecasts, now one of the most frequented sites on the net. Most smart people and boaties in particular will have an app to keep themselves right up to the minute with the latest coastal water forecasts.

Impressive waves are readily observed throughout Bass Strait and the Southern Ocean. Whether it be the huge seas that can crash into Cape Bridgewater and the blowhole, the relentless swell that marches in from South America towards Stokes Point at the southern tip of King Island, or the full force surf that endlessly moves onto Gunnamatta, ocean swell is ever present in this region. Interestingly, a wave rider buoy, located south of Stokes Point recorded a 27 metre wave a number of years ago. That is enormous by any standards.

Waves are to be respected at all times. I remember surfing at Waratah Bay, in South Gippsland when we noticed some fishing boats in close to the shore, near breaking surf. One of these boats was way too close to shore. The next thing, the boat had flipped. Skipper and crew were thrown into the water, with cooler late autumn water temperatures. Some of the fishing party had been drinking and we ended up driving one of the crew to Foster Hospital. This boatie was suffering from abrasions and mild hypothermia. Fortunately, all turned out well.

Surfing at 'Big Left', out from the golf course at Flinders, some years ago,

I 'survived a 15 foot 'monster' that came through and washed upwards of 20 surfers towards the shore. This event helped me to develop a healthy respect for 'rogue waves' that ceaselessly hit our shores.

Another point of interest in this part of the world is moderating influence of the sea and air temperatures. Most people immediately think that by going south to Tasmania and the Bass Strait islands you will be subjected to cooler air. After all it's closer to Antarctica. During the winter months I've observed that it can be appreciably colder in Melbourne than out at King or Flinders Islands, especially overnight. With the seawater acting as a huge store of thermal energy, temperatures rarely go below 12 degrees. Sure, there are the occasional frosts, but it's certainly colder in country Victoria or even Alice Springs during the winter nights.

*Weathers: My good friend Ian, a former lighthouse keeper at Deal Island, Cape Nelson, Cape Schanck and Gabo Island tells me they used to take the 'weathers': recording all the data from the meteorological instruments. I like the sound of this term which is yet to be found in any regular dictionary.

Bass Strait has been referred to as the 'eye of the needle'. "Wind funnelling occurs when weather systems, particularly coming in from the south west and south are deflected around Cape Grim and the north western part of Tasmania. By the time the wind hits the Furneaux Group the wind direction has changed from southwest to northwest, which is the prevailing wind direction at Flinders Island. Fishermen I have spoken to over the 30 years of my visitations to the 'Furneaux Group have referred to this funnelling; 'it blows harder and longer eastern Bass Strait.' This phenomenon is best witnessed by observing the Bureau of Meteorology website when rain is on the radar screen. The rotation through 90 degrees of direction is plainly evident with this modern observational weather technology.

Believe it or not, one of the windiest places in South-Eastern Australia may

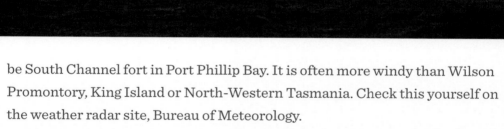

be South Channel fort in Port Phillip Bay. It is often more windy than Wilson Promontory, King Island or North-Western Tasmania. Check this yourself on the weather radar site, Bureau of Meteorology.

My most recent observation of roll or arcus cloud occurred late in the summer of 2015 in northern Bass Strait. Preceding a cold front, this spectacular cloud formation, resembling a tube of cloud or a 'bull nosed veranda' spanned more than one quarter of the sky. Viewed through binoculars, some of the constituent clouds resembled the Crab Nebula with particularly intricate shapes, one part of the cloud formation showing four distinct fingers. As the roll cloud started to break up other clouds took on more of a splashed appearance rather than the more smoothly shaped and rounded forms associated with more common clouds. Visit http://en.wikipedia.org/wiki/Arcus_cloud

Yachts and Model Boats

Smaller varieties are more manageable. Our first find was at North East River, at the top end of Flinders Island. A child's yacht that had blown away in gusts of wind, much the worse for wear. Our neighbour, Ian, set about re-masting the find and we completed the job with some improvised sails.

Hand made model courtesy Oakridge Holiday Home, Tasmania.

Found objects. Yacht from North East River. Furneaux Group, Tasmania.

Zostera Grass and Other Seaweeds

Unavoidable along any coastline, seaweed, the 'pasture of the sea' will be there to greet us. Shoreham on the southern Mornington Peninsula, has been a favourite location for gardeners who are searching for 'raw fertiliser for their gardens. After windy weather, the shores of Port Phillip Bay will yield their produce, usually the more delicate sea grasses. The kelps and bubble weed, usually being confined to the more exposed coastal and ocean areas, can make their presence felt after stormy weather.

At King Island, in Western Bass Strait, 'kelpers' (seaweed farmers with permits to collect the valuable booty) set about their work with an assortment of trucks, winches, trailers and 4WD utilities. The kelp factory located at Currie, is a thriving industry that exports the dried bull kelp to locations as far away as Scotland.

Tanners Bay at Flinders Island is another location where 'drifts' of seaweed can pile up along the shoreline. Depending upon prevailing winds and tides, small mounds of the sea grass can be almost impossible to climb or scale, being

Drying Bull Kelp, Currie, King Island.

well over one metre in height. Smaller mounds can make wonderful soft seats for beach walkers as they take a break from fossicking.

Some of my best cray diving spots have been draped in bubble weed and other weedy camouflage, making for a secretive and secluded abode for these bottom dwellers. Alas, the spirited free diver makes his presence felt in the pursuit of a handsome trophy, the Southern Rock Lobster.

Some years ago at Tanners Bay, a favoured spot for the paper nautilus shells, a local was reported to have seen a cray walking out of the water near these banks of seaweed, in pursuit of a tasty morsel of nautilus. Now I would not normally believe that the southern rock lobster would ever leave the briny for the land but a similar incident happened at Fingal Beach, Cape Schanck. A cray was literally walking on the rock platform, in the air and well away from the sea. Naturally, we gave this fish a better home.

Unusual seaweed ball, Discovery Bay National Park, Western Victoria.